RECIPES FROM A
SLOVENIAN
KITCHEN

RECIPES FROM A
SLOVENIAN KITCHEN

Explore the authentic taste of an undiscovered
cuisine in over 60 traditional dishes

JANEZ BOGATAJ

Photography by Martin Brigdale

This edition is published by Aquamarine,
an imprint of Anness Publishing Ltd, Blaby Road, Wigston,
Leicestershire LE18 4SE; info@anness.com

www.aquamarinebooks.com; www.annesspublishing.com

If you like the images in this book and would like to investigate
using them for publishing, promotions or advertising, please visit
our website www.practicalpictures.com for more information.

© Anness Publishing Ltd 2013

A CIP catalogue record for this book is available from
the British Library.

Publisher: Joanna Lorenz
Editorial Director: Helen Sudell
Project Editor: Emma Clegg
Designer: Gabriella Le Grazie
Illustrator: Robert Highton
Photography: Martin Brigdale
Food Stylist: Fergal Connolly
Prop Stylist: Helen Trent
Translator: Ana Hazler

PUBLISHER'S NOTE
Although the advice and information in this book are believed to
be accurate and true at the time of going to press, neither the
authors nor the publisher can accept any legal responsibility or
liability for any errors or omissions that may have been made nor
for any inaccuracies nor for any loss, harm or injury that comes
about from following instructions or advice in this book.

NOTES
• Bracketed terms are intended for American readers.
• For all recipes, quantities are given in both metric and imperial
measures and, where appropriate, in standard cups and spoons.
Follow one set of measures, but not a mixture, because they are
not interchangeable.
• Standard spoon and cup measures are level. 1 tsp = 5ml,
1 tbsp = 15ml, 1 cup = 250ml/8fl oz.
• Australian standard tablespoons are 20ml. Australian readers
should use 3 tsp in place of 1 tbsp for measuring small quantities.
• American pints are 16fl oz/2 cups. American readers should use
20fl oz/2.5 cups in place of 1 pint when measuring liquids.
• Electric oven temperatures in this book are for conventional
ovens. When using a fan oven, the temperature will probably
need to be reduced by about 10–20°C/20–40°F. Since ovens
vary, you should check with your manufacturer's instruction
book for guidance.
• The nutritional analysis given for each recipe is calculated per
portion (i.e. serving or item), unless otherwise stated. If the recipe
gives a range, such as Serves 4-6, then the nutritional analysis
will be for the smaller portion size, i.e. 6 servings. The analysis
does not include optional ingredients, such as salt added to taste.
• Medium (US large) eggs are used unless otherwise stated.

CONTENTS

Geography and landscape

Slovenia is a small country, and yet it is full of hidden delights. Anyone who is interested in beautiful countryside, fine historical castles and towns, winter sports, summer walks and delicious cuisine will find something here to relish. The Slovene people proclaimed their independence at the end of the 20th century after centuries under the domination of other countries. But, throughout the years, one thing they have never rejected is the culinary tradition of invading forces. Instead, they have always happily combined many different elements from abroad with their own native recipes to make a fascinating blend of European, Slavic and Central European tastes – even, after World War II, including some flavours from the Far East.

The shape of the country

Slovenia is bordered by four countries. First, Italy to the north-west, then moving clockwise, Austria to the north, a short border with Hungary to the east and a much longer one with Croatia to the south. The last and tiniest section of its border claims a mere 46.6 km/ 29 miles of coastline, which is tucked into a bay in the Adriatic, squeezed between Italy in the north and Croatia in the south. This gives the Slovenes precisely 2.5cm/1in of coastline per inhabitant, although there are enough Italian and Croatian seaports close by to supplement the catches made from the few small fishing towns on the Slovene coast – a fortunate situation, because the Slovenes greatly enjoy their fish and shellfish.

This is a desirable corner of Europe, sitting on the trading routes between East and West from pre-Roman times. Geographically, too, Slovenia is marked by the meeting points of four distinct regions: the Julian and Kamniske-Savinja Alps and the Karavanke mountains to the north, beyond which lies Austria; the Pannonian plains to the east, a wilder land of forests and fields where the river Danube flows through the fertile Hungarian plains; another mountain range, the Dinaric Mountains (Alps), to the south, wriggling its way down the coastline through Croatia; and finally, the warmer, flatter lands of the border with northern Italy, reaching around past Trieste to the Venetian lagoon.

Landscape and agriculture

Slovenia's countryside has a natural fertility. The warm south-facing lower slopes of the mountain ranges to the north are ideal places to grow fruit trees (especially apples, pears and plums), to raise animals for meat and dairy products, and, of course, to produce the excellent local wine. Where the land is lower-lying, the country is covered with forests full of game, lakes containing several varieties of freshwater fish, plus fields of cereal crops and grass for pasture. In the warmer west, more Mediterranean crops such as olives, figs and wine grapes can be grown, and much is made of the harvest from the sea.

The countryside is so thickly forested, however, that agriculture is a relatively minor part of the Slovene landscape. Only in the north-east is there room for large fields of grain; elsewhere the main products are those grown on a small scale, such as grapes, apples and plums, and small numbers of poultry. Cattle, sheep and

LEFT The island on Lake Bled in north-western Slovenia with mountains behind.

LEFT A hillside farm and vineyard at Jeruzalem, near Ljutomer, Stajerska, in the north-east of the country.

to eat fresh seafood such as mussels or squid, or tasty pizza – a Slovene favourite in this corner near Italy.

Typical climates

Though small, Slovenia enjoys three distinct climates. The mountains to the north experience cold winters and pleasantly warm summers, with beautifully fresh air and clear mountain streams. Here vineyards thrive with their faces towards the sun all day.

In the flatter eastern plains and river valleys bordering Hungary and Croatia, the central European climate of freezing winters and hot dry summers is the norm. This area is perfect for growing summer crops, and raising cattle and pigs to be slaughtered and preserved for the cold winter months. It also boasts many vineyards.

Finally, in the western coastal area bordering Italy and the Croatian coast, temperatures are warmer overall, with cool winters and hot summers, similar to those in Italy. Here there is more of an outdoor lifestyle, with food such as spicy kebabs, pancakes and pastries enjoyed in open-air cafés and eateries.

pigs are found in the Alps and the central regions of the country. Many farmers still raise their own pigs, which traditionally have provided them with enough cured meat for cold winters.

Tourist attractions

With such great natural resources, Slovenia has turned to tourism as a major source of income. Well before the 21st century, Slovene spas were a favourite of the well-heeled European looking for a change of scene and a cleansing diet. Whether these cured the liverish 18th-century nobleman is unclear, but they are still popular today.

Slovenia is the perfect place to go to see mountains, fields, forests, lakes and rivers all in one day. This is a small country, and so from the centrally placed capital, Ljubljana, it is only a short drive north to the mountains of the Julian Alps where the energetic tourist can ski or hike, then try local sweet cakes and doughnuts. The Slovenes are very proud of their mountains – the highest peak, Triglav, is 2,864m/9,396ft and dominates the northern border.

To the south-west lies the famous Karst limestone plateau and the forests along the Croatian border. There are amazing caves beneath the plateau,

RIGHT Slovenia is a mountainous republic and almost half of the land is forested.

and here, the famous beautiful white Lipizzaner horses are bred, often performing for visitors. Tourists may be tempted to buy the famous cured ham (pršut), which is air-dried rather than smoked, and cured by the strong wind that blows over the Karst plateau.

It is another short drive north-east to the picturesque medieval villages and castles of eastern Slovenia. This white wine-producing area also comprises many spa towns based around health-giving mineral springs.

Finally, to the far west is the pretty coastline and the Soca valley, where the Soca river wriggles its way down the Italian border. This is the best place

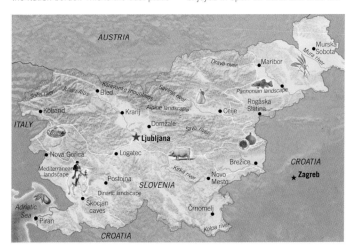

Slovene culture

The national identity of Slovenia has been fiercely defended by its people since the Dark Ages. Although the country has spent most of its history under the government of other countries and empires, Slovene customs and traditions have always been prized. While there may have been some resentment at the long domination by outside forces, this does not mean that the locals resented the food and drink brought in from surrounding areas; indeed, it is another Slovene tradition to welcome new tastes and cooking techniques and, if possible, to grow the ingredients needed for these exciting recipes in their fertile soil.

The peasant tradition

From the 14th century to the 20th century, Slovenia was ruled by the governments of the Holy Roman Empire as well as the Austro-Hungarian Empire under the Habsburgs. The Slovenes fought off the Turks, who threatened to march in from the south-east, preferring Austro-Hungarian dominance from the north.

Slovenia had then a peasant economy. Peasant farmers lived on a subsistence diet of locally grown produce, most of which went to pay the lord of the manor, or was given to the Catholic church and its monasteries. This is one reason why white (wheaten) bread is so highly valued in Slovenia, even today – it is a symbol of the comfortable life to which many peasants could only aspire. The best white flour always went to the rich, so white bread became a treat to be made into elaborate loaves for special occasions. These still form the centrepiece of family feasts at Easter, Christmas and birthdays of note.

Staple ingredients

The peasants lived on legumes such as lentils and peas, grains such as barley and millet, vegetables, honey and dairy products, and a small amount of meat. As in other European countries, the slaughter of the family pig for winter food (koline) became a ritual celebrated by friends and family. Nothing was wasted from the animal, hence the famous Slovene cured meat and sausages, as well as the stews and hotpots that use a small amount of meat or offal in inventive ways.

Slovenes also happily embraced the food of the invading forces. Ingredients such as potatoes, which found their way to Slovene farms at the end of the 18th century, were adopted with great enthusiasm and now form a staple part of the diet throughout the country. Corn and buckwheat were even earlier imports, and had a profound effect on the recipes for pites (pies), flat cakes and dumplings, which are such a speciality of Slovenia.

Structure of Slovenia since 1991

As Slovenia is situated at the northern edge of the former communist Yugoslav Federation, just next to independent Austria and Italy, it was the first of the ex-Communist states to gain independence in 1991 and join the EU and NATO, even deciding to move to the euro as its only currency.

There is considerable pride that Slovenia led the way into the EU, forging a path that has since been followed by other Eastern European countries. When each member nation was invited to contribute a cake to celebrate the 50th birthday of the EU

LEFT Slovene street musicians playing the accordion.

in 2007, the sweet-toothed Slovenes offered not one but two typical cakes to delight: a pehtranova potica (sweet bread roll with tarragon and nuts) and a prekmurska gibanica (apple strudel with poppy seeds and curd cheese).

Religious traditions

The predominant force in religious life in Slovenia is Catholicism. Throughout its history until the arrival of Communism in 1945, Slovenia always embraced the public rituals of the Roman Catholic Church. From 1945–91, public rituals were banned and went underground. But somehow, the rituals of religious feasts lived on. Today, now that people are free to choose their own religion, there has been a revival of all the old customs: Christmas, Shrovetide, Easter and various saints' days, each with dishes that make for a splendid feast.

Monasteries have been a fixture of Slovene life since at least the 13th century. Monks have traditionally

ABOVE The white, blue and red national flag of Slovenia first appeared in 1848.

been supported by contributions of food from local people, as well as growing their own produce and producing their own medicines.

ABOVE A peasant chapel at the roadside near Celje, a city in central Slovenia.

Ethnic influences

Over 83 per cent of citizens claim to be ethnic Slovenes; the rest are from Italy, Hungary or the Balkan states (Serbia, Croatia and Bosnia). So you find many of the characteristic dishes of the neighbouring Balkan states (burek), with their tradition of grilled (broiled) and spiced meats (čevapčiči, ražnjiči, pleskavica), and the Italian diet of pizza and pasta. With the fantastic heritage of regional dishes and foods from these immigrant traditions, Slovenia can truly claim status as a culinary empire.

This might suggest that Slovenes import many ingredients. Nothing could be further from the truth: Slovenes are far more likely to use home-grown ingredients than other European countries, delighting in adapting recipes and adopting farming techniques so that, for example, home-grown sautéed potatoes can reign supreme for a traditional Slovene Sunday lunch.

LEFT Cows grazing in the Alps, in the north-west of the country.

Festivals and celebrations

In a country where the preparation and discussion of food is such a major part of life, it is no surprise that the rituals connected with religious festivals and family celebrations should be based around eating and drinking. Religious feasts were discouraged during the Communist era in the second half of the 20th century, and the food traditions associated with them were kept alive in the privacy of people's homes. This economically vibrant country also revels in newer traditions, such as birthday parties, and hen and stag parties before weddings, all of which involve large quantities of food and drink and an immense amount of planning.

Christmas

In Slovenia, Christmas is celebrated in style in every home, with the family gathered together – the more involved, the merrier.

At Christmas, the preparations begin well before the actual day. Christmas fairs are a popular event around the country, starting off the festive atmosphere from the end of November onwards. The cooking begins in earnest a few days before Christmas Day, when the centrepiece of the celebrations, the potica (a rolled bread filled with all kinds of good things – spices, fruit or nuts) is prepared and baked. On Christmas Day itself, families will gather after church for a lavish meal with several courses, lasting the rest of the day. A Slovene wine usually accompanies the meal, and brandy comes later. If anyone has room, there may be more cakes in the evening.

Shrovetide

Before the Easter feast comes the Lenten period of fasting. At Shrovetide, the few days just before Lent, people focus on cooking filling and fatty treats to last them through the lean days to come. Cakes such as krofi (fried doughnuts) are central to Shrovetide.

In the old days, the last fatted pig on the farm might be killed at this time to keep the family and their friends going with good meat over the final days of winter, and the best cuts would be eaten first as roasts and stews, before the lesser cuts were cured and made into sausage. This was an occasion for all the inhabitants of the village to meet up at the farm in the hope of partaking in a filling treat.

Easter

Celebrations during the Easter period are even more elaborate than at Christmas. The food is based around bread once again, with another version of potica as the main dish. However, at Easter there are also the decorated hens' eggs that are so common in all European countries as a symbol of fertility and the coming spring. These eggs have different names in the various regions of Slovenia – pisanice, pisanke, pirhi, remenke, remenice – and families enjoy playing games with them, such as the traditional egg hunt, which so delights children.

Saints' days

Celebrated throughout the year, saints' days are often linked to the changing seasons. Towards the end of winter, St Valentine's Day on 14 February and St Gregory's Day on 12 March both anticipate the coming of spring.

LEFT The fearsome and imposing Kurenti are the most popular figures in Shrovetide carnivals. They are believed to drive away winter and bring spring into the countryside.

Bread again forms a major part of the festivities, with special little loaves in the shape of birds placed in the trees to encourage the birds to wake up and begin mating. These bird loaves were often collected by the children in rural areas and kept to eat for breakfast, soaked in warm milk, when there was nothing else in the larder.

St George's Day on 23 April also focuses on the renewal of spring, and eggs are eaten in the form of jurjevo cvrtje (St George's scramble), a dish that is shared by all the inhabitants of each village.

Autumn festivals include All Saints' Day and St Martin's Day, on 1 and 11 November, when children go from house to house collecting buns (vahči). In harder times, these buns would have been stored away to keep families fed during the long, cold nights of winter.

A goose is often roasted on St Martin's Day to commemorate the saint, who is reputed to have hidden among a flock of geese before he accepted the post of bishop. St Martin's Day is also the principal celebration day for wine – something the locals enjoy partaking in alongside delicious feast dishes.

BELOW Slovenes celebrating the Summer Arts Festival in Ljubljana.

Weddings

During previous centuries, Slovene weddings were a much more elaborate affair than they are now. There would be feasts and drinking on at least three separate occasions: once at the first meeting between the two families, when they negotiated the terms of the marriage; again at the engagement; and finally, at the wedding itself.

Nowadays things are less formal, with the wedding day being the main focus of attention. At the ceremony itself, the priest will still bless a bottle of good wine, and then share it with the bride and groom in the church.

The wedding feast is often a proper dinner with several courses. The focus, as at Christmas and Easter, is on an elaborate bread loaf, often made to look like a plaited heart, which all the guests will share. It is a Slovene tradition for the guests to bring all the sweet elements of the feast – cakes, pastries and puddings – which will be distributed at the end of the celebrations. There is also a large, rich wedding cake, which is cut at midnight by the bride and groom together, as in many other countries.

Christenings

It is only fairly recently that Slovenes have celebrated a christening with food as well as drink. In previous centuries, it was more common for the

ABOVE This photograph from between the wars shows traditional Slovenian costume.

godparents and the midwife to drink the baby's health at a local inn. However, nowadays a christening is another good excuse for a party, often held at a restaurant. The bread tradition continues here too, with the godparents presenting the baby's family with a pure white loaf, plain or plaited, to symbolize good luck and good health for the child.

Funerals

After someone has died, the feasting goes on. Families and friends in Slovenia will happily discuss funerals in terms of what was eaten and drunk at the wake (pogrebščine), rather than dwelling on the sadness of the occasion. The deceased person used to be laid out at home for seven days so that people could pay their respects, and of course all these visitors had to be fed.

These days, the whole ritual is more likely to take place in a funeral parlour, where a lot of people will visit and will expect to be given food and drink. Many funeral parlours have kitchens and a room where the visitors can gather to chat among themselves, while eating snacks or even whole three-course meals. Of course, they will also toast the deceased with wine, beer or brandy.

The Slovene cuisine

Slovene farmers have always made the most of their natural resources, right back to the days when peasants lived mainly on lentils and peas, grains such as barley and millet, and dairy products. For many years the peasants were kept in relative poverty, while their best produce paid the rent. Luckily, Slovenia is a country with a fertile soil and a good climate for agriculture. Once farmers began to cultivate the land, most people's daily diet became much more varied. Still, every part of the food available was used, and one can see in many recipes today the survival of an old tradition of filling, starchy grain and vegetable dishes, with all kinds of meat added in small quantities.

Daily food

Breakfast in Slovenia is usually a simple affair consisting of coffee, bread rolls or pastries filled with jam, and sometimes cheese, particularly in the rural areas where a farmer might still make his or her own delicious sharp cheese from cow's or sheep's milk.

At lunchtime, everything stops for a good long three-course lunch, the main meal of the day. As with all meals in Slovenia, it is important to choose the food carefully and discuss it afterwards. There will usually be soup, followed by a meat or fish dish with plenty of potatoes, pasta or noodles and a salad, and then a dessert – strudel is the favourite.

The evening meal tends to be a somewhat shorter version of lunch, with one or two courses, based around salads as a refreshing end to the working day, and maybe eating up any leftovers from midday. During the week, midday meals may be relatively simple affairs of two or three courses, but at weekends, the Slovene habit of constructing more complicated dishes to enjoy with the whole family requires real dedication from the family cook. It is not unknown for old-fashioned recipes to require three or four separate types of cooking, for example making a meat mixture, a vegetable mixture, and a sauce, and finally combining them in a baked dish.

Festive menus

Holiday meals are even more elaborate, with many courses – at least six for an Easter Sunday feast. The culture of sharing dishes means that many people can try everything on the table, which encourages spirited conversation and a friendly discussion of the various recipes.

No wonder many Slovenes like to escape to a restaurant for weekend meals, particularly Sunday lunch.

The country is peppered with inns called *gostilna*, where you can buy a superb and filling meal. Both locals and tourists like to make their way to a *gostilna*, usually out in the country or on the outskirts of the main towns, so that they can linger over a good solid three-course lunch with some Slovene wine or beer, and perhaps a speciality fruit brandy to finish.

Specialities of Slovenia

The development of a national Slovene cuisine is bound up with its history as a trading nation and a tourist destination. As far back as the 6th century, Slavic immigrants settling in Slovenia found a population of peasant farmers with

BELOW FAR LEFT This breakfast feast shows curd with fruit jam and bread.
BELOW LEFT Traditional Slovene cheese.
BELOW Raw, air-dried ham, or kraški pršut, on display in a butcher's shop.

their own cuisine, and an expertise in dairy farming and cheese making. This interest in cheese and other dairy products is a mainstay of the cuisine in Slovenia, even today.

Other ingredients arose from the local climate. Where better to grow grapes for wine than the gentle slopes of the Alps, where the vines face the sun almost all day, but temperatures are not hot enough to scorch them in the summer? Slovene wine is also well known outside the country, although it does deserve a wider recognition for its quality. Brandy, too, often flavoured with the local fruits – apples, pears and herbs from the forest – is a favourite drink to end a meal.

Fruits of land and sea
The forests that cover much of the country yield their earthy mushrooms, and rich game such as pheasant, hare or wild boar to be made into a tasty casserole. A few bears and wolves hide in these primeval forests, and many species of plants and flowers that are extinct elsewhere in Europe still grow here in the untouched undergrowth.

The wind that whips down the karst limestone plateau in the west has proved a bonus. The local air-dried

meats, such as sausage and ham, develop a particular flavour from this form of preservation. Elsewhere in the country, meat is smoked to preserve it for winter, and smoked pork sausages are very popular in cold weather.

Over in the far west of the country, the sea and its produce has more of an influence on local tastes. There are many tasty fish recipes in Slovenia, both for freshly caught seafood and for the freshwater trout from the rivers and lakes, which are often served dusted with cornflour (cornstarch) and roasted whole to seal in the flavour.

Foreign influences
Slovenia in the 21st century is still accumulating culinary ideas and expertise from abroad. Many restaurants have adopted the Balkan habit of spicing meat with paprika and grilling (broiling) it as steaks or kebabs. These barbecued dishes are immensely popular, especially for an outdoor meal on a summer's evening. As it has in much of Europe, Italian pizza has swept the nation, with its great flavours and speed of cooking – a concept quite different to the traditionally more elaborate Slovene cuisine. Chinese food has also become

ABOVE LEFT Guests sitting in front of a restaurant in Ljubljana.
ABOVE A dish being prepared by a waiter in a restaurant in Ptuj.

very popular in Slovenia, again with the influence of a new wave of immigrants from the East.

Slow food groups
As a contrast to all this new speedy cooking, some Slovenes have developed their local versions of the 'slow food' groups that originally started in Italy. In a rebellion against the trend to prepare, cook and eat food quickly, the splendidly titled 'Society for the Recognition of the Sautéed Potato as an Independent Dish' was formed in 2002 in Ljubljana. Its numbers have grown, and other groups have started up with the same ethos – to ensure that proper time and care is given to food.

The sautéed potato has been a staple of a proper Slovene Sunday lunch since this humble vegetable was brought to the country back in the 18th century. In a country where food is a major topic of conversation between families, friends, neighbours and work colleagues, it is no wonder this movement is successful.

Classic ingredients

Slovene cuisine is a great melting-pot of traditions. The country's cooks have always concocted delicious meals from all kinds of regional ingredients, as well as wholeheartedly accepting new tastes and methods of cooking from abroad. Even with the latter, Slovenes like all the ingredients to be readily available locally, and nearly everything is made fresh.

Seasonings

A vital part of the Slovene cuisine is careful seasoning, using spices, herbs and other flavourings to enliven the basic ingredients. Some of these are native to Slovenia, and others have been brought in by invaders over the centuries and adopted by local cooks.

Pepper Hot red pepper (chilli) and mild red pepper (paprika) arrived in the country with the Turks in the 16th century. Paprika is the main seasoning in goulash, a favourite dish for a warming winter supper.
Cinnamon This aromatic flavouring is used in many of the cookies, cakes and pastries so beloved of the Slovenes.
Poppy seeds The Eastern European tradition of sprinkling bread and cakes with poppy seeds is very common in Slovenia. A particular favourite is potica,

the rolled and stuffed sweet or savoury bread that forms the centrepiece of Christmas and Easter feasts, and often has poppy seeds in the fillings.
Honey The main sweetener for centuries over the whole of Europe, before sugar arrived from the East in the 12th century. Honey is still highly prized in Slovenia and many small farmers keep bees.
Horseradish This is a classic element of many a meat dish in Slovenia. Its sharp taste makes a great foil for boiled beef in particular. It also forms part of the ritual of any Easter feast, representing the nails of Christ's cross.
Herbs Slovene recipes use a lot of fresh herbs, according to what is available at a particular time of year. Tarragon is a favourite, with its sharp taste enlivening both potica and struklji (dumplings). Many other herbs are

found in Slovene dishes, including basil, bay leaf, thyme, dill, chives, marjoram and mint.
Flavoured oil and vinegar The flavour of a dish can be lifted by using a flavoured oil or vinegar as an extra seasoning, either as a dressing or during cooking. Apple and wine vinegar are commonly found in salad dressings, particularly in dishes containing sauerkraut. Pumpkin oil is a great favourite that dates back to the earliest days of agriculture in the country. Olive oil is also widespread in Slovenia, and oil from six different types of local olive tree adds a distinctive flavour to salads and vegetables.

Meat and poultry

Roasts and stews, cured ham and tripe – all kinds of meat form the bulk of the main course in Slovenia. Even in the

BELOW Sugar was often scarce, and honey is still produced by many Slovenes.

BELOW Horseradish forms part of the Easter dinner of ham, eggs, bread and potica.

BELOW The cuisine is distinguished by meat, with smoked gammon a popular choice.

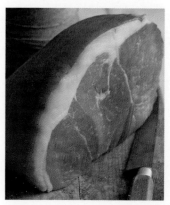

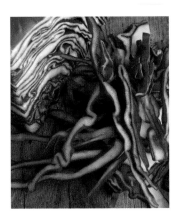

ABOVE Slovenia is well known for its semi-dried, lightly smoked sausages.

ABOVE Pike is available in the many freshwater lakes around the country.

ABOVE Red cabbage is most often eaten braised, traditionally with a roasted goose.

days when meat was scarce in the rural areas, dinner would usually contain a morsel of bacon or a pig's trotter (foot) for flavour.

Pork The pig was the mainstay of Slovene cuisine for centuries. Many small farmers kept their own pig to slaughter in the winter and share with family and friends, and every scrap was used. The most famous Slovene meat dish is smoked sausage (kranjska klobasa), a strong and tasty product that can be added to all sorts of savoury recipes or simply eaten sliced with sauerkraut or salad and a glass of wine. Cured ham is a speciality of the Karst region, where it is hung outside to dry in the biting wind rather than being smoked. Once all the meat of the pig has been eaten, the fat is rendered to use as lard in cooking other dishes. Even after the rendering process, thrifty cooks would save the tiny scraps of meat remaining in the fat and use them as a savoury stuffing for a rolled potica.

Beef The finer cuts are found simply fried as steak. The lesser cuts make a very tasty soup, often with the addition of homemade noodles for bulk.

Tripe An acquired taste to most people these days, tripe is still popular in Slovenia. It is bought pre-cooked or gently simmered in a savoury sauce until it is really tender.

Poultry Chicken, duck, goose and turkey feature in many dishes. Like the family pig, poultry could be raised in small quantities on a peasant's strip of land. It can be roasted, then the scraps are used for meat loaf, or added to soups such as chicken noodle.

Fish and shellfish
Inland, the fast-flowing rivers and placid lakes contain delicious freshwater fish, and all along the west side of the country, the sea is never far away.

Freshwater fish Pike, carp and trout from the rivers and lakes are usually oven-baked, sometimes with spices like a fish goulash, or covered with a sour cream sauce. The local trout, Salmo trutta marmoratus (soška postrv), is an indigenous variety only found in this area.
Sea fish White fish steaks are often marinated and baked with vegetables. Firm-fleshed halibut is also made into kebabs sold as street snacks, after it has been marinated in onion, lemon and olive oil for a lovely fresh taste.

Shellfish Squid, calamari, mussels and other shellfish should be eaten really fresh, so they tend to be found in the port towns along the Adriatic, gently fried or cooked in white wine.
Salt cod (stockfish) This method of preserving cod is used in many European countries. Salt cod needs a bland accompaniment, such as polenta or potatoes. It must be soaked first and the soaking water discarded several times before it is ready to cook.

Vegetables and salads
The Slovenes have always made the most of produce from the land. Vegetables feature in every meal, raw or cooked, simply boiled or baked in delicious combinations.

Potatoes The potato has been enthusiastically adopted by the Slovenes since its introduction in the 18th century, and is now a symbol of the national cuisine. Simple dishes such as sautéed potatoes abound as accompaniments to meat or fish dishes. There are also more elaborate recipes such as potato dumplings, or hotpots with other vegetables such as cabbage, baked in the oven in stock or milk.

ABOVE Gathering wild mushrooms in Slovenia's many forests is a popular pastime.

ABOVE Dandelion leaves are used in salads and the shoots are considered a delicacy.

ABOVE The preference for sauerkraut shows the Austro-German influence of the cuisine.

Cabbage and pickled cabbage (sauerkraut) Spicy sauerkraut has become a mainstay of Eastern European cuisine. Its sharp taste adds piquancy to many a meat or fish dish, and livens up salads and plainer vegetables. Sauerkraut blends well with meat and vegetables in a sour soup to make a great pick-me-up, with sour cream stirred in just before serving. White or red cabbage in its fresh form is also a Slovene favourite, and is used as a main ingredient in soups, hotpots and other baked dishes, or simply added raw to salads.

Mushrooms The beautiful dense forests that cover much of Slovenia yield good crops of mushrooms of all kinds. They are cooked as side dishes, or added to a stew for a dark rich flavour, or they may also be made into snacks with melted cheese.

Beans and peas From the earliest days of Slovene history, legumes such as beans, peas and lentils were grown to provide a source of protein for the hungry farm workers. These worthy vegetables are still enjoyed as part of a warming soup or stew, perhaps with some added pork sausage or pasta to make it even more filling.

Root vegetables Carrots, turnips and mangelwurzels (mangold) are commonly used as accompaniments to main courses of meat or fish, often grated raw and coated with a flavoured oil and vinegar dressing. Their bland flavour absorbs the spicier taste of the dressing, and they are also found with sauerkraut as a side dish, to offset its piquant flavour.

Onions and shallots These strong, tasty vegetables are used in many a Slovene recipe. Onions make a great stock for soup, and are an essential part of goulash, adapted from the Hungarian classic. They can also be fried as an accompaniment to a spicy kebab. The milder, sweeter shallots are found in fish dishes such as Piran baked fish.

Cucumber and other salads Salad vegetables of all varieties are very popular in Slovenia, and none more so than the humble green cucumber. It has a subtle flavour that blends very well with oil and vinegar or creamy salad dressings, particularly those based on sour cream.

Garlic This strong and flavoursome vegetable adds piquancy and brings out the flavour of many savoury dishes. The influence of Italian cuisine is obvious in the use of garlic in vegetable stews such as ratatouille, as well as meat hotpots.

Fruit and nuts

The fresh, sharp taste of fruit is an essential part of Slovene desserts and cakes. Nuts, in particular walnuts, blend well with fruit and add a distinctive flavour to sweet and savoury dishes.

Lemons and oranges These sharp citrus fruits have been used as flavourings for cakes and cookies for centuries. Christmas cookies use the aromatic zest of lemons and oranges to cut through the sweetness of dates, honey and candied fruit.

Apples These are the basis for a favourite Slovene sweet dish, apple strudel. Apples can also be added to a fruit salad, served stewed, hot or cold, or they can be baked in batter for a more filling pudding.

Olives Plump olives can be grown in the far west of the country, on the borders with Italy where a balmy Mediterranean climate is enjoyed. They are generally made into oil, either for cooking or for making salad dressings with a special cider or wine vinegar. Olives and their oil have many health-giving properties.

Figs These sweet fruits, with their distinctive taste and crunchy seeds, are often dried and added to special bread and cakes at Christmas or Easter.

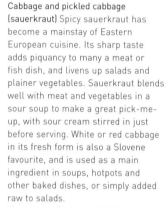

Walnuts A special favourite, walnuts are the main flavouring in the Christmas sweet bread, potica. They are used whole, chopped or ground, often blended with honey or sugar syrup, as their taste can be rather strong.

Other nuts Hazelnuts, pine nuts and sweet chestnuts are native to this part of Europe. Chestnuts help to bulk up any vegetable casserole, and were once a mainstay of the country cook needing to feed farm workers in the winter.

Barley, wheat, rice and other grains
The diet of the peasants who worked the land in earlier centuries relied heavily on the staple food of filling grains. Today, a basic grain porridge is still enjoyed by Slovenes, alongside more elaborate sweet and savoury dishes that are based on these solid health-giving and versatile ingredients.

Barley and millet These two grains were a staple food of the farm workers in Slovenia from the Middle Ages onwards. They are made into tasty casseroles and soups by blending them with any available vegetables, and maybe adding a scrap of meat for flavour. At their most basic, barley and millet make a sustaining porridge that is still popular today.

BELOW Apple sauce is an essential component of many Slovene recipes.

Buckwheat This strong-tasting grain was brought to Slovenia in the 15th century, and today it is made into all manner of dishes, including pancakes, cheesecakes, dumplings, polenta, porridge and hotpots.

Wheat and corn (maize) These two grains were traditionally ground into the finest white flour, which was claimed by the lord of the manor as rent from the peasant farmers. These days, white bread is still highly prized in Slovenia and forms the central part of many celebratory meals. Nothing is wasted from a white loaf of bread: even when it is stale, it makes fantastic breadcrumbs to top baked vegetable dishes and roasted fish.

Rye As in many parts of Europe, rye flour is used to make loaves of rich, strong-tasting, dark bread – sometimes with added caraway – a great contrast to the pure white loaf made of wheat. Rye bread is often eaten at breakfast time, and is often topped with homemade jam.

Rice Mixed with beans in a savoury casserole, rice makes a sustaining protein-rich meal. With the addition of milk, sugar and cinnamon, it becomes a filling and delicious pudding that is often served chilled and garnished with a sprinkling of nuts.

BELOW Curd cheese is used in savoury and sweet breads, pastries and soups.

Dairy products
Eggs, cheese and cream, especially sour cream, are used in many Slovene recipes. These dairy products were available for most of the year on small-sized farms and added essential protein to dishes such as soups, vegetable stews and desserts.

Eggs Hens are, of course, kept for their eggs as well as for meat. There are several popular egg dishes in Slovenia, such as the dish from Ljubljana containing white bread, hard-boiled eggs and mushrooms.

Cheese Both sweet and savoury recipes use a soft curd (farmer's) cheese, such as in buckwheat cheesecake, or the simple starter of curd cheese with onion. Curd cheese is often part of the filling for a bread roll (potica), served with poppy seeds or aromatic fresh herbs such as tarragon.

Cream and sour cream Another favourite dairy product, sour cream is added to soup just before it is served, and, of course, it always tops any goulash. Adding a dab of sour cream is a great way to embellish any bland recipe with a sharper taste. The plainer taste of fresh cream makes it ideal for adding to potato and vegetable dishes, and as a filling for sweet pastries.

BELOW Grains used in Slovenia include barley and millet, buckwheat and rye.

Filo pastry

Filo or štrudel pastry is used widely in Slovene desserts, including the national favourite, Prekmurje Gibanica Pie. The homemade variety is not as difficult to make as it looks. This pastry doesn't need gentle handling; the more you bash the dough, the more flexible it will be. It does need careful rolling out on a very large work surface until almost transparent. Prepare the filling ingredients before you start rolling: the pastry must be used immediately for best results.

Makes about 275g/10oz

225g/8oz/2 cups strong white
   bread flour
2.5ml/½ tsp salt
1 egg, lightly beaten
10ml/2 tsp sunflower oil
about 150ml/¼ pint/⅔ cup slightly
   warm water

1 Sift the flour and salt into a mixing bowl and make a well in the centre. Stir the egg and oil into the water, add to the flour and mix thoroughly to form a sticky dough.

2 'Beat' the dough by lifting it and slapping it down on a lightly floured surface. Continue until the dough no longer sticks to your fingers, then knead for 5 minutes until it feels smooth and elastic. Shape the dough into a ball, place it on a dish towel and cover with an upturned bowl.

3 Leave the dough to rest in a warm place for about 30 minutes.

4 Lightly flour a very large clean cloth, such as a tablecloth, and roll out the dough as thinly as possible, lifting it frequently to prevent it from sticking.

5 Gently stretch the dough with your hands spread out flat underneath it. Work around the dough, stretching it until it is paper-thin and forms a square about 65cm/26in. Trim off the thick edges with scissors.

BAKING FILO PASTRY

Filo pastry must never dry out, or it will become brittle and hard to fold and shape. Keep the sheets you are not working with covered with a damp dish towel. It may also crumble if it is too cold so, if it has been refrigerated, remove and allow to stand for 1 hour.

Filo must always be lightly brushed with melted butter before baking to give it a shiny glaze – unsalted butter is perfect because it has a lower water content, or oil can also be used. The fat should be brushed as evenly and thinly as possible to create light crisp layers. Never brush filo with egg or milk as this would make it too soggy.

The usual temperature for baking filo pastry is 200°C/400°F/Gas 6, although it can be cooked at a slightly lower temperature without its crisp texture being affected. It colours quickly, so check frequently towards the end of the cooking time. If the pastry has browned before the filling is cooked, cover loosely with foil, and remove for the last few minutes.

TOTAL AMOUNT: Energy 895kcal/3790kJ; Protein 27.4g; Carbohydrate 174.8g, of which sugars 3.4g; Fat 14.5g, of which saturates 2.7g; Cholesterol 190mg; Calcium 344mg; Fibre 7g; Sodium 77mg.

Mlinci

Serves 4–6
400g/14oz/3½ cups plain white
    (all-purpose) flour
2 eggs, lightly beaten
a little water
50g/2oz/½ cup pork crackling or cooked
    diced bacon

A side dish for poultry and meat dishes, mlinci are also served as a main dish with cream or butter, or topped with curd cheese and poppy seeds. They may be drizzled with honey for a sweet dessert.

1 Sift the flour into a bowl. Make a well in the middle and add the eggs, then gradually work in the flour to make a firm dough, adding just enough water to bind the ingredients.

2 Knead the dough until smooth, then cut it into four equal portions. Roll each into a large circle, about 3mm/⅛in thick.

3 Heat a griddle or heavy frying pan so that it is warm, but not too hot. Dry out the circles of dough slowly, turning once, until they are crisp and pale golden on both sides. Transfer the circles to a wire rack and leave to cool.

4 To serve the mlinci, break them into pieces, put them in a large bowl and pour in boiling water. Leave for about 10 minutes. Drain the mlinci and serve topped with crackling or bacon.

Bread dumplings

Serves 4
15ml/1 tbsp sunflower oil
1 onion, very finely chopped
1 egg, lightly beaten
45ml/3 tbsp milk
45ml/3 tbsp chopped fresh parsley
115g/4oz/2 cups fresh
    white breadcrumbs
salt and pepper

Slovenes are devotees of dumplings, or kruhovi cmoki, which are eaten every day in some households. They are served as an accompaniment to soups and stews, such as goulash, or as an appetizer, tossed in a little melted butter and topped with chunks of crispy bacon.

1 Heat the sunflower oil in a frying pan, add the onion and then cook over a low heat, stirring frequently, for about 10 minutes or until softened, but not coloured.

2 Meanwhile, place all the remaining ingredients in a bowl and stir together. Leave this to soak for a few minutes.

3 Add the onion to the soaked breadcrumb mixture and season generously with salt and a few twists of ground black pepper. Stir together until the ingredients are thoroughly mixed.

4 With damp hands, shape the dumpling mixture into 12 walnut-sized balls. Add them to a soup, casserole or gently boiling water or stock, cover and simmer for about 15 minutes or until the dumplings are cooked. Serve immediately.

MLINCI PER SERVING: Energy 270kcal/1143kJ; Protein 9.7g; Carbohydrate 51.8g, of which sugars 1g; Fat 4.1g, of which saturates 1.2g; Cholesterol 68mg; Calcium 103mg; Fibre 2.1g; Sodium 154mg.
BREAD DUMPLINGS PER SERVING: Energy 159kcal/672kJ; Protein 5.8g; Carbohydrate 24.3g, of which sugars 2.4g; Fat 5.1g, of which saturates 0.9g; Cholesterol 48mg; Calcium 84mg; Fibre 1.4g; Sodium 245mg.

APPETIZERS
AND SOUPS

Curd Cheese with Onion

Cucumbers in Cream

Crackling Flat Cakes

Pork in Aspic

Vegetable Soup

Mushroom Soup

Bean Soup

Sour Pork Soup

Chicken Noodle Soup

Sunday Beef Broth

Succulent appetizers to savoury soups

The cold winters and hot summers of Slovenia call for appetizers to suit both chilly and warm days. Soups are great favourites, especially during the winter months. These are often based on meat or poultry with homemade noodles or dumplings added as a substantial garnish. The goodness of locally grown vegetables and herbs comes to the fore in hot soups, such as tasty bean soup fižolova juha, sharpened with vinegar and sour cream for a filling dish, and in cold appetizers, such as cucumbers in cream, in which the piquant flavours of buttermilk and sour cream counteract the bland taste of the vegetables. After a hot day in the baking sun, a cooling bowl with fresh bread goes down well.

Crackling flat cakes – little baked cakes of thick dough with salty pork pieces – are a popular snack to accompany a drink, and tasty spreads such as curd cheese with onion complement a crunchy, rustic loaf beautifully. These spreads are ideal to serve as appetizers before a hearty casserole or a roast meat, or they can be served on their own as a light lunch.

Serves 4
450g/1lb/2 cups homemade or bought
   curd (farmer's) cheese
5ml/1 tsp paprika
1 onion, finely chopped
30ml/2 tbsp pumpkin seed oil
salt and ground black pepper

Curd Cheese with Onion
Koroška skuta s čebulo

Used to fill savoury and sweet breads, packed into pastries, added to soups or turned into delicious desserts, curd cheese is a much-loved ingredient in Slovenia. This recipe is popular as a first course in the northern region of Carinthia. Flavoured with onion and paprika, and drizzled with pumpkin seed oil, it tastes good with rye bread (see page 122).

1 Put the cheese into a bowl. Add the paprika and a little salt and pepper to taste. Mix together with a wooden spoon, then stir in the onion.

2 Drizzle the pumpkin seed oil all over the spread and serve with black rye bread or pumpernickel.

COOK'S TIP
To make curd (farmer's) cheese, rinse a large heavy pan with cold water. Pour in 2 litres/3½ pints/8¾ cups fresh whole milk. Put over a high heat and bring to a rapid boil. When the milk starts to froth up, turn the heat to low and drizzle in 30ml/2 tbsp fresh lemon juice. Gently stir until large lumps of soft curd form. If this doesn't happen within a minute, return the pan to the heat, stir in another 15ml/1tbsp lemon juice. When curds have formed, set aside the milk for 10 minutes. Line a colander with muslin (cheesecloth) and scald with boiling water. Gently pour the milk through. Gather the corners of the cloth around the curds and tie together. Rinse in cold water and leave to drain for several hours. Turn the cheese into a bowl, cover and chill until ready to use.

PER SERVING: Energy 207kcal/859kJ; Protein 17.1g; Carbohydrate 5.6g, of which sugars 4.8g; Fat 14.7g, of which saturates 6.5g; Cholesterol 27mg; Calcium 137mg; Fibre 0.2g; Sodium 494mg.

Serves 6
1kg/2¼lb cucumbers
1 small onion, very finely chopped
750ml/1¼ pints/3 cups
    buttermilk, chilled
250ml/8fl oz/1 cup sour cream, chilled
3 garlic cloves, finely chopped
pinch of ground cumin
salt and ground black pepper
ground cumin, to garnish

Cucumbers in Cream
Smetanove murke

Slovene summers are mostly dry with temperatures averaging 20–30°C (68–86°F). This refreshing cold dish from north-east Slovenia is a cross between a drink and a soup and was once an essential feature of country life with summer days spent working in the fields. Slices of crusty krusna pec (rustic white bread) make a good accompaniment.

1 Peel and grate the cucumbers and place in a bowl. Sprinkle with salt and add the finely chopped onion, then cover and set aside for about 30 minutes. The salt will draw out some of the juices from the cucumber.

2 Squeeze the cucumber and onion and drain it thoroughly in a sieve (strainer). Alternatively, leave the cucumber to drain in the sieve and then squeeze out the water by pressing gently.

3 Mix the garlic, cumin and pepper into the buttermilk and stir in the sour cream, mixing well.

4 Stir in the cucumber and onion mixture and then serve immediately by ladling into chilled bowls and sprinkling with some ground cumin.

COOK'S TIP
If you can't get buttermilk, stir 15ml/1 tbsp lemon juice into 750ml/1¼ pints/3 cups semi-skimmed milk and leave it to stand for 30 minutes before using.

PER SERVING: Energy 152kcal/631kJ; Protein 7.3g; Carbohydrate 11.5g, of which sugars 10.1g; Fat 8.9g, of which saturates 5.4g; Cholesterol 30mg; Calcium 225mg; Fibre 1.4g; Sodium 78mg.

  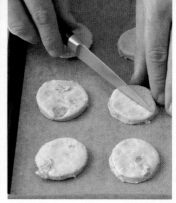

Crackling Flat Cakes
Ocvirkove pogačice

These tasty little savoury cakes are especially popular in the north-eastern region of Prekmurje, where they are commonly served as a snack with drinks, usually white wine. They are delicious eaten while they are still quite warm from the oven, and also make a wonderful appetizer before a main meal.

Makes about 20
300g/11oz/2¾ cups self-raising (self-rising) flour
250g/9oz pork crackling, chopped
2 egg yolks
45ml/3 tbsp white wine
1 egg yolk, to glaze
salt

1 Preheat the oven to 180°C/350°F/Gas 4. Grease two baking trays with vegetable oil. Place the flour in a bowl and stir in the pork crackling with a pinch of salt (use less if the crackling is already salty). Make a well in the middle of the mixture and then add the egg yolks and wine.

2 Stir the yolks and wine together with a fork, then mix all the ingredients together, using the fork at first and then bringing the mixture together gently with your hands to make a dough.

3 Place the dough on a floured surface and roll it out swiftly and lightly until it is about 5mm/¼in thick. Use a biscuit (cookie) cutter or glass to stamp out 3–5cm/1¼–2in circles. Gather the trimmings together, re-roll and cut out more cakes. Carefully transfer the cakes to the baking trays, spacing them 2.5cm/1in or so apart to allow room for them to spread and rise.

4 Use a small sharp knife to lightly score the surface of the cakes. Make a glaze by lightly whisking the egg yolk with a few drops of cold water. Brush the glaze evenly over the cakes, then bake in the preheated oven for about 15 minutes, until lightly browned, risen and just firm.

5 Leave on the baking trays for a couple of minutes, then lift them on to a wire rack to cool slightly – these are best served while still warm.

COOK'S TIP
Ocvirki, the crisp brown residue of rendered pork, or crackling, feature in many savoury Slovene recipes. If you haven't the time or inclination to prepare them yourself, packets of pork scratchings are the perfect alternative.

PER SERVING: Energy 129kcal/540kJ; Protein 6.3g; Carbohydrate 11.4g, of which sugars 0.2g; Fat 6.6g, of which saturates 2.2g; Cholesterol 43mg; Calcium 56mg; Fibre 0.5g; Sodium 55mg.

Serves 6
4 pig's knuckles and trotters (feet)
1 pig's ear (optional)
1 onion, sliced
3 garlic cloves, sliced
1 bay leaf
1 fresh thyme sprig
1 fresh marjoram sprig
5ml/1 tsp black peppercorns
salt

VARIATION
To make clear aspic, pour the strained stock into a clean pan. Add 1 egg white and whisk over a low heat until frothy. Stop whisking, then boil gently with the frothy crust. Remove from the heat before the crust breaks and let the froth subside. Repeat twice. Scald a sieve (strainer), muslin (cheesecloth) to line it, and a bowl. Strain the stock through the lined sieve into a bowl. It should now be crystal clear.

Pork in Aspic
Žolca

Popular throughout Slovenia, this is a traditional way of using pork knuckle and trotters. The meat is cooked and finely chopped, then set in tasty jellied stock or aspic to make a delicious snack. Traditionally, this dish is thickly sliced and served with cider vinegar and black rye bread.

1 Place the meat in a large pan or stockpot and cover with cold water. Bring slowly to the boil, skimming off any scum. Reduce heat and simmer for 10 minutes, until the scum stops rising.

2 Add the onion, garlic, bay leaf, thyme, marjoram, peppercorns and a good pinch of salt. Leaving the lid off, simmer gently for about 3 hours, or until the meat is falling off the bones.

3 Lift the pork out, gathering any pieces of meat that have fallen off the bones. Remove and discard the skin and bones, and chop the meat finely. Place in a shallow dish. Set aside.

4 Return the bones to the stock, and boil until reduced to about half, leaving enough to cover chopped meat. Strain stock into a jug (pitcher), set aside until cool, but not setting.

5 Season the stock and pour over the meat. Cover and chill overnight, until the stock has set to a jelly. Cut into thick slices. Eat within 2–3 days.

PER SERVING: Energy 249kcal/1036kJ; Protein 29g; Carbohydrate 0.8g, of which sugars 0.6g; Fat 14.4g, of which saturates 5.3g; Cholesterol 88mg; Calcium 12mg; Fibre 0.1g; Sodium 1085mg.

Serves 4

1kg/2¼lb mixed fresh vegetables
   in season
25g/1oz/2 tbsp butter or 30ml/2 tbsp
   vegetable oil
1 onion, chopped
115g/4oz/⅔ cup lean smoked
   bacon, diced
3 potatoes, peeled and grated
30ml/2 tbsp chopped fresh parsley
salt and ground black pepper
sour cream, to serve (optional)

VARIATION

For a more substantial soup, stir in a
200g/7oz can of drained and rinsed
cannellini or red kidney beans. This is
delicious served with bread dumplings
(see page 19) or a loaf of freshly baked
crusty white bread or rolls.

Vegetable Soup
Zelenjavna juha

Many households have their own vegetable plot and grow
a large selection of fresh produce all year round.
Favourites include cabbages, turnips, leeks, carrots,
celery, cauliflower and green beans. This richly flavoured
chunky soup makes a satisfying appetizer – or it can be
served for lunch with some warm crusty bread.

1 Peel or prepare the vegetables and
dice them into small chucks.

2 Melt the butter or heat the oil in a
large pan and add the onion. Cook
gently, stirring occasionally, for about
10 minutes, until softened. Add the
bacon and cook, stirring, for 5
minutes, until both the onion and
bacon are lightly browned.

3 Add the mixed vegetables and pour
in enough water to cover. Bring to the
boil, then reduce the heat and cover
the pan. Simmer for 5 minutes.

4 Add the potatoes, bring the soup
back to the boil and simmer for a
further 10 minutes, or until all the
vegetables are tender.

5 Taste and season the soup with salt
and pepper, then stir in the chopped
parsley and serve by ladling into
warmed bowls. Serve each portion
with a small spoonful of sour cream,
if you like. This creates a delectable
contrasting flavour.

PER SERVING: Energy 295kcal/1234kJ; Protein 8.9g; Carbohydrate 41.3g, of which sugars 21.2g; Fat 11.5g, of which saturates 2.8g; Cholesterol 15mg; Calcium 95mg; Fibre 8g; Sodium 523mg.

Serves 6

3 potatoes, peeled and diced
2.5 litres/4¼ pints/10⅔ cups water
7.5ml/1½ tsp parsley leaves
2 garlic cloves, crushed
1 bay leaf
1 fresh thyme sprig
30ml/2 tbsp lard, white cooking fat or oil
1 small onion, finely chopped
115g/4oz fresh wild mushrooms (such as ceps, chanterelles or mixed mushrooms), finely sliced
30ml/2 tbsp plain (all-purpose) flour
cider vinegar, to taste
sour cream, to garnish (optional)
salt and ground black pepper

Mushroom Soup
Gobova juha

Slovenia is rich with mushrooms and they feature in many dishes, including this simple wholesome soup, delicious served with a dollop of sour cream.

1 Place the potatoes in a large pan and pour in the water. Add the parsley, garlic, bay leaf and thyme. Bring to the boil, reduce the heat and cover the pan, then simmer for 20 minutes, until the potatoes are tender.

2 Meanwhile, heat the lard or oil in a pan and add the onion. Cook, stirring occasionally, until the onion is golden. Add the mushrooms and continue to cook, stirring gently until they are reduced and the juices they yield have evaporated.

3 Stir the flour into the mushrooms and then ladle in some of the potato stock. Stir until smooth, then add the mushrooms and all the liquid from the pan to the potatoes.

4 Add a little vinegar to taste, then simmer the soup for 15 minutes. Season with salt and serve garnished with a little sour cream added to each portion, if you like.

VARIATION
Many large supermarkets now sell a range of wild mushrooms. If you can't find any, substitute cultivated varieties such as chestnut and shiitake.

PER SERVING: Energy 115kcal/482kJ; Protein 2.4g; Carbohydrate 18.2g, of which sugars 1.8g; Fat 4.1g, of which saturates 0.5g; Cholesterol 0mg; Calcium 16mg; Fibre 1.3g; Sodium 11mg.

Serves 6

350g/12oz/2 cups dried red
    kidney beans
1 bay leaf
1 fresh or dried rosemary sprig
1 garlic clove, chopped
¼ lemon
30ml/2 tbsp lard, white cooking fat or oil
1 small onion, chopped
30ml/2 tbsp plain (all-purpose) flour
vinegar or dry white wine, to taste
salt and ground black pepper
45ml/3 tbsp sour cream, to garnish

Bean Soup
Fižolova juha

This hearty soup is perfect for the cold, damp days of winter. It is very easy to prepare, although you do need to pre-soak the dried beans overnight. Serve sprinkled with buttery fried breadcrumbs, chunks of black rye bread and a tall glass of cool beer.

1 Soak the beans overnight in plenty of cold water. Drain and place in a large pan with boiling water to cover. Bring to the boil and boil for 10 minutes. Drain and return the beans to the pan with fresh boiling water.

2 Tie the bay leaf and rosemary together and add to the pan with the garlic and lemon. Bring to the boil, reduce the heat, cover and simmer for 1 hour, or until the beans are soft.

3 Drain the beans, reserving the liquid. Discard the herbs and lemon, and mash the beans until smooth.

4 Heat the oil or melt the lard in the rinsed-out pan. Add the onion, then cover and cook gently for 10 minutes, until softened but not browned. Stir in the flour and cook, stirring, for a minute. Then stir in the beans and cooking water to thin the soup.

5 Bring to the boil, stirring all the while, and simmer for 5 minutes, adding more cooking liquid, if necessary, to thin the soup. Stir in a little vinegar or wine to sharpen the soup and season to taste. Add the sour cream just before serving.

PER SERVING: Energy 224kcal/947kJ; Protein 13.7g; Carbohydrate 30.7g, of which sugars 2.4g; Fat 6.1g, of which saturates 1.5g; Cholesterol 5mg; Calcium 75mg; Fibre 9.5g; Sodium 14mg.

Serves 6

400g/14oz boneless pork and offal
  (variety meats), including lung or
  lights, stomach or tripe, and heart
2–2.5 litres/3½–4¼ pints/8¾–10⅔
  cups water
1 bay leaf
4 fresh thyme sprigs
5ml/1 tsp cumin seeds
2 garlic cloves, chopped
15ml/1 tbsp lard, white cooking fat or
  vegetable oil
1 onion, chopped
15ml/1 tbsp plain (all-purpose) flour
2.5ml/½ tsp paprika
cider vinegar or dry white wine, to taste
salt and ground black pepper
thyme leaves, to serve

Sour Pork Soup
Štajerska kisla juha

This pork soup, which contains a little cider vinegar or
dry white wine, is traditionally the final dish served at
wedding reception meals, usually after midnight.

1 Dice the meat and offal into small
pieces and place in a large pan. Pour
in the water and bring slowly to the
boil, skimming off any rising scum.

2 Reduce the heat so that the water
barely simmers, add the bay leaf,
thyme, cumin and garlic. Cover and
simmer gently for 1 hour, until the
meat and offal are tender.

3 Heat the lard or oil in a separate
pan and add the onion. Cook, stirring
often, for about 10 minutes, until the
onion is soft but not browned. Stir in
the flour and paprika to make a smooth
paste. Cook, stirring, for 1 minute.

4 Remove the pan from the heat.
Gradually add a ladleful of liquid from
the soup, stirring to make a smooth
thin paste. Stir the mixture into the
soup and bring to the boil, stirring
continuously. Remove the bay leaf
and the thyme stalks.

5 Add salt, pepper and cider vinegar
or dry white wine to taste, garnish
with thyme leaves and serve.

PER SERVING: Energy 104kcal/436kJ; Protein 13.3g; Carbohydrate 3g, of which sugars 0.6g; Fat 4.6g, of which saturates 1.1g; Cholesterol 47mg; Calcium 12mg; Fibre 0.2g; Sodium 51mg.

Serves 6
1.5kg/3¼lb chicken, jointed into 8 pieces
1 onion, trimmed and thickly sliced
1 bouquet garni (parsley, thyme and
   bay leaf tied together)
5ml/1 tsp cider vinegar
1 green (bell) pepper, cored, de-seeded
   and chopped
115g/4oz/1½ cups button (white)
   mushrooms, halved
175g/6oz/1½ cups green peas
225g/8oz egg noodles
15g/½oz/1 tbsp butter
30ml/2 tbsp chopped fresh chives
salt and ground black pepper

Chicken Noodle Soup
Piščančja juha z rezanci

This delicious meal-in-a-bowl combines tender poached chicken, tasty vegetables and soft egg noodles in a flavoursome clear stock. A little butter and fresh chives stirred into the soup at the last minute will add the final finishing touch to this simple meal.

1 Rinse out the chicken and remove any pieces of fat from the inside. Put the chicken, onion slices, bouquet garni and vinegar in a large pan and cover with cold water. Slowly bring to the boil, skimming off any rising scum. Reduce the heat, cover and gently simmer for 1 hour, or until the chicken is tender.

2 Remove the chicken from the stock and leave until cool, then cut off the meat, discarding the skin and bones. Cut into bitesize pieces.

3 Strain the stock, discarding the onion and bouquet garni. Pour back into the cleaned out pan and add the green pepper and mushrooms. Bring back to the boil and simmer for 10 minutes, then add the chicken, peas and noodles. Simmer for a further 5 minutes, or until the vegetables and noodles are tender.

4 Season the soup with salt and a twist of black pepper to taste. Stir in the butter and chives, then ladle into warmed bowls to serve.

PER SERVING: Energy 399kcal/1680kJ; Protein 41.1g; Carbohydrate 32.1g, of which sugars 3.2g; Fat 12.7g, of which saturates 4.8g; Cholesterol 149mg; Calcium 30mg; Fibre 3.1g; Sodium 195mg.

Sunday Beef Broth
Goveja juha

Beef broth, flavoured with vegetables, herbs and saffron, is usually served at Sunday lunchtime, garnished with little bread dumplings (see page 19), fine egg noodles or small pastry shapes known as bleki. The tender braised beef that flavours the soup is then served as the main meal. Serve with slices of crusty white bread.

Serves 6

450g/1lb beef or veal bones
1kg/2¼lb stewing beef, in one piece
2–2.5 litres/3½–4¼ pints/8¾–10⅔
    cups water
½ onion, peeled
2 carrots, cut into chunks
1 celeriac, cut into chunks
½ swede (rutabaga), cut into chunks
1 ripe tomato, halved
½ small red (bell) pepper, seeded
    and sliced
1 parsley root, scrubbed, with leaves, or
    1 large bunch of parsley with stalks
1 garlic clove, sliced
1 bay leaf
6–8 black peppercorns
pinch of saffron threads
salt

COOK'S TIP

Peel off just the outer layer of papery skin from the onion and trim off the root, but leave on the inner orange-brown skin because this will help to colour and flavour the soup.

1 Use a meat cleaver to chop up any larger bones (or get your butcher to do this for you) to impart the maximum flavour during cooking. Put them in a stockpot or large pan with the beef.

2 Pour in the cold water, add salt to taste and bring the pan slowly to the boil. Do not remove the foam from the surface of the soup during cooking – this contributes to the final flavour.

3 Meanwhile, brown the cut side of the onion in a dry non-stick frying pan or griddle until light brown in colour, then turn it and brown the other side.

4 Add the onion, carrots, celeriac, swede, tomato and red pepper to the stockpot. Bring this to the boil, then reduce the heat, so that the liquid barely simmers. Cover and cook for 2½–3 hours or until the beef is tender.

5 Add the parsley root or bunch of parsley (tied with string), garlic, bay leaf and peppercorns for the final 15 minutes cooking.

6 Turn the heat off and leave the pan to stand for 5 minutes, then skim any foam and fat from the surface. Lift the beef from the soup and transfer it to a serving platter. Cover and keep in a warm place until ready to carve and serve. Discard the bones from the soup.

7 Meanwhile, pound the saffron into a fine powder in a small mortar using a pestle, then stir in a little of the hot soup to dissolve the spice. Strain the broth and stir in the saffron.

8 Reheat the broth and taste, then adjust seasoning as necessary before serving with little bread dumplings or noodles.

PER SERVING: Energy 317kcal/1324kJ; Protein 38.6g; Carbohydrate 5.3g, of which sugars 5g; Fat 15.8g, of which saturates 6.4g; Cholesterol 97mg; Calcium 56mg; Fibre 1.8g; Sodium 121mg.

ONE-POT MEALS

Warming stews and hearty medleys

The Slovene habit of cooking hearty, filling and delicious meals in one pot harks back to the days when the peasant farmers of the region cooked everything together in a large cooking pot on the stove or in the oven. These hotpots are generally best left to simmer very slowly – a method of cooking that retains the flavour and juiciness of all of the tasty ingredients.

One-pot meals usually contain a combination of meat and vegetables, and a filling starch such as potatoes, rice or pasta. Busy cooks juggling families and jobs will be pleased that there is no need to serve anything else with these dishes – all the goodness of the vegetables is retained in the delicious gravy. A little preparation and the pot can be left to cook itself.

Grains such as barley, buckwheat, rice and millet are the staples of Slovene cooking. Beans and root vegetables make a nutritious base to absorb flavours of small amounts of meat. Finally, stocks often include a dash of tangy cider vinegar or sauerkraut, plus some sour cream to serve.

Serves 4
8 small turnips
50g/2oz/½ cup millet flakes
salt and ground black pepper
butter, to garnish

VARIATION
For a richer stuffing, add 30ml/2 tbsp
curd (farmer's) cheese to the cooked
millet before stuffing turnips.

Millet-stuffed Turnips
Loška smojka

With their crisp ivory flesh and slightly peppery flavour, these humble root vegetables are
delicious prepared by hollowing out and filling with a savoury stuffing, then slowly baked.
In the past, the stuffed turnips would have been prepared in the morning and left to simmer
gently all day long in the cool oven of a kitchen range.

1 Preheat the oven to 180°C/350°F/
Gas 4. Trim the roots and tops from
the turnips, and carefully scrub them,
then hollow out the centre of each.
Place the turnips in an ovenproof
dish or a small roasting pan, so that
they are a single layer deep.

2 Place the millet flakes in a pan and
add just enough water or vegetable
stock to cover, then bring to the boil
and cook for 5 minutes, until the
water is absorbed but the millet is
not completely cooked. Season with
salt and pepper. Divide the millet
among the turnips, spooning it into the
hollows and pressing it down neatly.

3 Pour in some boiling water to
surround the vegetables almost up
to their tops. Cover the dish, using
foil if necessary. Bake for about
1 hour, or until the turnips are
completely tender and the millet is
swollen and cooked.

4 Drizzle melted butter over the
stuffed turnips and serve at once.
They are delicious with red wine.

PER SERVING: Energy 68kcal/290kJ; Protein 1.9g; Carbohydrate 15.2g, of which sugars 4.5g; Fat 0.5g, of which saturates 0g; Cholesterol 0mg; Calcium 51mg; Fibre 2.4g; Sodium 16mg.

Serves 6

500g/1¼lb/3 cups dried beans, such as
    red kidney or cannellini beans
100g/3¾oz rindless smoked streaky
    (fatty) bacon, diced
1 onion, chopped
2 cloves garlic, crushed
500ml/17fl oz/generous 2 cups
    well-flavoured vegetable stock
15ml/1 tbsp tomato purée (paste)
500g/1¼lb potatoes, diced
500g/1¼lb sauerkraut, drained and
    briefly rinsed in cold water
salt and ground black pepper

Bean and Sauerkraut Hotpot
Jota

Pronounced 'yota', Jota is a renowned dish that comes from the Primorska region, close to the Adriatic Sea. It's a thick, smoky-flavoured, sweet and sour hotpot, delicious served with a glass of cviček – a light red wine, unusually made from a blend of red and white grapes. Slices of crusty white bread make a good accompaniment.

1 Soak the beans overnight in plenty of cold water, then drain and place in a pan with plenty of fresh cold water. Bring to the boil and boil rapidly for 10 minutes, then reduce the heat and simmer for about 45 minutes, or until the beans are tender. Drain the beans and set aside.

2 In a large pan, heat the bacon gently until the fat runs. Add the onion and garlic, and cook until the onion is lightly browned and the bacon is well cooked. Stir in the stock, tomato purée, potatoes, sauerkraut and cooked beans.

3 Bring to the boil, then reduce the heat, cover and simmer for 15 minutes or until the potatoes are very tender and the mixture is thick. Stir in the beans and simmer for a further 2–3 minutes. Taste for seasoning before serving.

VARIATION
Instead of sauerkraut, many traditional Jota recipes are made with 'kisla ripa': pickled or 'sour' turnip.

PER SERVING: Energy 339kcal/1436kJ; Protein 23.6g; Carbohydrate 52.2g, of which sugars 5g; Fat 5.4g, of which saturates 1.6g; Cholesterol 11mg; Calcium 134mg; Fibre 16g; Sodium 732mg.

Pork and Vegetable Stew
Šara

Pork is the most popular meat throughout all Slovenia, and no part of the pig is wasted as this tasty dish demonstrates – although you can substitute stewing pork, if you prefer. The stew contains a delicious and nutritious mixture of root vegetables, which are harvested in late autumn and stored away for the colder months. A warming horseradish sauce and sumptuous rye bread (see page 122) are the usual accompaniments, although a colourful green vegetable would also be good.

Serves 4

2 pig's trotters (feet), chopped in half
1 fresh pig's tail, chopped into portions
1 pig's ear, chopped in half
1 bay leaf
5ml/1 tsp dried thyme
5ml/1 tsp dried rosemary
5ml/1 tsp dried marjoram
5ml/1 tsp ground cumin
2 garlic cloves, peeled
60ml/4 tbsp cider vinegar
4 carrots, cut into chunks
1 celeriac, cut into chunks
1 swede (rutabaga), cut into chunks
1 leek, sliced
1 onion, quartered
500g/1¼lb potatoes, thickly sliced
bunch of fresh parsley, trimmed
    and chopped
salt and ground black pepper

To serve

horseradish sauce
black rye bread or pumpernickel

1 Place the trotters, tail and ear in a large stockpot. Add just enough water to cover the meat and bring to the boil. Remove the scum that surfaces.

2 Add a good pinch of salt, plus the bay leaf, thyme, rosemary, marjoram, cumin, garlic and the 30ml/2 tbsp vinegar. Bring back to the boil, reduce the heat and cover the pan. Leave it to simmer for 1¼ hours.

3 Add the chopped and sliced carrots, celeriac, swede, leek, onion, potatoes and parsley. Bring back to the boil, then reduce the heat and cover the pan once more. Add about 1 litre/1¾ pints/4 cups water. Simmer for another 10 minutes.

4 Remove the meat from the pan and cut into bitesize chunks, discarding the skin and bones. Return the meat to the stew and cook for a final 10 minutes, or until the vegetables are tender when pierced with a fork.

5 Taste and season with a little salt and ground black pepper, if needed, and add a little more vinegar, if you like. Ladle on to warmed plates or into bowls and serve accompanied by horseradish sauce and black rye bread.

COOK'S TIP
To allow the flavours to develop, make the stew the day before, cool and chill in the refrigerator overnight. The following day, remove any solidified fat from the top, then gently reheat the stew in a pan until it is piping hot and bubbling before serving.

PER SERVING: Energy 472kcal/1980kJ; Protein 39.1g; Carbohydrate 43.2g, of which sugars 23.2g; Fat 17g, of which saturates 5.6g; Cholesterol 107mg; Calcium 192mg; Fibre 9.7g; Sodium 717mg.

Serves 4–6

115g/4oz/⅔ cup dried red kidney beans
30ml/2 tbsp olive or vegetable oil
150g/5oz smoked bacon or smoked
    ham, diced
1 bay leaf
1 onion, chopped
1 garlic clove, crushed
15ml/1 tbsp tomato purée (paste)
25g/1oz/¼ cup plain (all-purpose) flour
600ml/1 pint/2½ cups ham or
    vegetable stock
150g/5oz pasta shapes
5ml/1 tsp dried marjoram
5ml/1 tsp ground paprika
5–10ml/1–2 tsp cider vinegar
salt and ground black pepper

VARIATION
For a meatier version, a piece of trimmed
bacon or gammon (smoked or cured ham)
can be simmered with the beans, then
diced and added when the pasta is cooked.

Bean and Pasta Hotpot
Pašta fižol

This warming winter combination of beans, cubes of
smoked bacon or ham and pasta is popular throughout
the Mediterranean region of Slovenia. Bursting with
rich flavours, it is finished with a dash of cider vinegar
and served with hearty black rye bread (see page 122).

1 Soak the beans overnight in plenty
of cold water. Drain them and place
in a large pan of fresh water, then
bring to the boil and boil for
10 minutes. Reduce the heat and
simmer for about 40 minutes, or until
the beans are just tender.

2 Heat the oil in a large pan and add
the bacon or ham, bay leaf and onion.
Cook, stirring occasionally, for about
15 minutes, until the bacon is cooked
and the onion is lightly browned.

3 Stir in the garlic and tomato purée.
Add the flour, a little at a time, then
gradually pour in the stock. Bring to
the boil, stirring until it is thickened.
Now add the pasta, marjoram and
beans, and simmer in the pan for
about 10–15 minutes or until the
pasta is tender and the sauce
has thickened.

4 Stir in the paprika, then add cider
vinegar, salt and pepper to taste.
Serve with buttered slices of black
rye bread or pumpernickel.

PER SERVING: Energy 547kcal/2319kJ; Protein 22.8g; Carbohydrate 96.9g, of which sugars 5.2g; Fat 10.4g, of which saturates 2.3g; Cholesterol 13mg; Calcium 61mg; Fibre 6.6g; Sodium 399mg.

Serves 6

30ml/2 tbsp olive oil

1 onion, chopped

1 slice pancetta or smoked
    bacon, diced

1 garlic clove, chopped

30ml/2 tbsp chopped fresh parsley

225g/8oz/1¼ cups long grain rice

500g/1¼lb hulled spring peas

salt and ground black pepper

shavings of Parmesan cheese,
    to garnish

VARIATION
For extra flavour, use vegetable or a light
chicken stock instead of the water and
stir in 15ml/1 tbsp curd (farmer's) cheese
or sour cream before sprinkling the top
with Parmesan shavings.

Rice and Peas
Riži biži

Some areas of Slovenia were once a part of Italy, and
this influence is clearly seen in pasta and pizza recipes
and in this classic rice dish, called 'risi e bisi' in Italian.
Risottos such as this one feature on many restaurant
menus and are flavoured in many ways, seafood being
especially popular. Here, it is made with long grain
rather than the more typical Arborio rice.

1 Heat the olive oil in a pan. Add
the chopped onion, pancetta or
bacon, garlic and parsley. Cook the
ingredients, stirring frequently,
until the onion is softened but not
quite browned.

2 Measure the volume of rice in a jug
(pitcher) or by the cup as you add it to
the pan, and then pour in half of the
volume of water. Bring to the boil,
reduce the heat and cover the pan.
Simmer for 10 minutes, until the rice
is partially cooked.

3 Add the peas, salt and pepper and
pour in some more water – about the
same volume as the first time. Then
bring the dish slowly back up to
simmering point.

4 Cover and simmer for a further
15 minutes or until the rice is tender
and the water is absorbed.

5 Serve the rice and peas hot in
pasta bowls or dishes, and sprinkle
each one generously with
Parmesan shavings.

PER SERVING: Energy 289kcal/1200kJ; Protein 11.5g; Carbohydrate 40.3g, of which sugars 2.6g; Fat 9.1g, of which saturates 2.1g; Cholesterol 11mg; Calcium 42mg; Fibre 4.4g; Sodium 213mg.

Serves 4

450g/1lb/2½ cups dried beans, such as
   cannellini or red kidney beans
1 bay leaf and a bunch of fresh parsley
675g/1½lb potatoes, quartered
25g/1oz/2 tbsp butter
120ml/4fl oz/½ cup sour cream
75g/2½oz/½ cup pork crackling or
   diced cooked bacon
2 garlic cloves, crushed
salt

Creamed Potatoes with Beans
Matevž

This dish is typical of the popular bean and potato dishes of central and south-eastern
Slovenia, and in some parts it is known as medved (bear). It is usually served with stewed
sauerkraut or sour turnip, with sausages or roast or smoked pork.

1 Put the beans into a large bowl,
cover with plenty of cold water and
soak for at least 5 hours, or
overnight. Drain the beans and place
them in a pan with plenty of fresh
cold water to cover them. Add the bay
leaf and parsley, and bring to the
boil. Boil hard for 10 minutes, then
reduce the heat and cover the pan.
Simmer for about 45 minutes, or
until the beans are tender. Drain well.

2 Cook the potatoes in boiling water
for 20 minutes, until tender. Drain
them and return them to the pan.
Add the butter, cream and beans and
mash the vegetables until smooth.
Alternatively, put them through a
potato ricer to make a smooth purée.

3 Stir in the crackling or bacon and
garlic with a little salt to taste, then
pile the mash into a bowl to serve.

COOK'S TIP
Most dried beans need to be boiled
rapidly for 10 minutes to remove harmful
toxins. This is particularly important for
red kidney beans, which can make you
very unwell if not treated in this way.

PER SERVING: Energy 602kcal/2541kJ; Protein 35.4g; Carbohydrate 77.7g, of which sugars 5.9g; Fat 18.8g, of which saturates 8.4g; Cholesterol 42mg; Calcium 163mg; Fibre 20g; Sodium 87mg.

Serves 4
250g/9oz/1¼ cups kasha (toasted
   buckwheat)
750ml/1¼ pints/3 cups vegetable stock
75g/3oz/6 tbsp butter
1 onion, chopped
500g/1¼lb mixed wild and/or
   cultivated mushrooms
60ml/4 tbsp chopped fresh parsley
250ml/8fl oz/1 cup sour cream
salt and ground black pepper

Buckwheat with Creamed Mushrooms
Ajdova Kaša z gobami

Buckwheat is an everyday food in many households in the central and alpine areas of
Slovenia. It may be served alone with butter, buttermilk or yogurt, or with a vegetable, such
as stewed sauerkraut or sour turnip, or as shown here, with wild mushrooms.

1 Put the kasha in a non-stick pan and
toast over a medium heat, stirring for
3–4 minutes, until it has become
slightly darker in colour. Turn down
the heat to very low. Carefully pour
over the stock, cover and simmer for
10–15 minutes, or until the kasha has
absorbed all the stock and is tender.

2 Melt the butter in a frying pan.
Add the onion and cook, stirring for
10 minutes until it is soft, but not
browned. Add the mushrooms and
cook, stirring frequently, until they
are lightly browned in places and
evenly cooked. The time will depend
on the type, so be careful not to
overcook any delicate mushrooms.

3 Add the parsley, cream and
seasoning to the mushrooms, then
heat for a few seconds. Add the
kasha, fork the ingredients together
lightly and serve at once.

COOK'S TIP
Kasha is the name for whole buckwheat
grains (often cracked) that have been
roasted. Crushed and hulled unroasted
buckwheat grains are used in porridge.

PER SERVING: Energy 436kcal/1808kJ; Protein 8.4g; Carbohydrate 36.7g, of which sugars 3.9g; Fat 29.3g, of which saturates 17.7g; Cholesterol 77mg; Calcium 115mg; Fibre 2.3g; Sodium 151mg.

Slow-braised Pork and Barley
Ričet

Believed to be the oldest cultivated grain, barley features in many recipes throughout central and Eastern Europe. Here, it soaks up some of the juices and thickens the rich gravy to make a hearty hotpot. There's no need to serve anything else with this dish because it makes a complete meal in itself. With this traditional fare, smoked pig's trotters are used, but meaty sausages would make an excellent alternative.

Serves 6
225g/8oz/1 cup pot barley
4 smoked pig's trotters (feet)
1.5 litres/2½ pints/6¼ cups water
1 garlic clove, crushed
1 leek, thinly sliced
1 bay leaf
225g/8oz shelled broad (fava) beans
3 potatoes, diced into large chunks
1 carrot, diced into large chunks
bunch of fresh parsley, trimmed
    and chopped
30ml/2 tbsp cider vinegar
salt and ground black pepper

COOK'S TIP
Pot barley is the whole grain with just the inedible outer husk removed and is available from larger supermarkets and health-food stores. Pearl barley is husked, steamed and then polished; it does not need pre-soaking.

1 Rinse the barley well, and then put it into a bowl, cover with plenty of cold water and leave to soak for at least 5 hours or overnight.

2 Place the pig's trotters in a large pan and pour in the water – it should generously cover the pork. Add a little more if needed.

3 Slowly bring the pan to the boil, skimming off any scum that rises to the surface. Reduce the heat slightly, so that the water boils steadily, and cook for an additional 45 minutes.

4 Drain the barley and add it to the pan with the crushed garlic, sliced leek and bay leaf. Bring the pan back to the boil, reduce the heat slightly, cover with a lid and cook for 15 minutes.

5 Add the beans, diced potatoes, diced carrot and most of the parsley (reserve a little parsley for garnishing when the dish is ready to be served).

6 Bring back to the boil, reduce the heat, cover and cook for about 30 minutes, until the meat, barley and vegetables are all tender when tested with a fork.

7 Lift the trotters out of the pan (keeping the rest of the hotpot on a gentle simmer), remove all the meat and cut into bitesize chunks.

8 Stir the vinegar into the hotpot and season to taste with salt and pepper. Ladle into bowls, top with the meat and sprinkle with the reserved parsley.

PER SERVING: Energy 344kcal/1452kJ; Protein 16.2g; Carbohydrate 51.4g, of which sugars 3.5g; Fat 9.6g, of which saturates 3.3g; Cholesterol 27mg; Calcium 48mg; Fibre 4.4g; Sodium 788mg.

VEGETABLES AND DUMPLINGS

One-pot Cabbage and Potatoes

Sautéed Potatoes

Wild Asparagus Omelette

Buckwheat Polenta with Celeriac

Cabbage with Noodle Squares

Braised Red Cabbage

Ljubljana Egg Dish

Gorica Chicory

Sauerkraut Salad

Buckwheat Dumplings

Idrija Potato Pockets

Tarragon Rolled Dumpling

Sautéed potatoes to sauerkraut

In common with most Europeans, Slovene cooks like to serve an inventive range of side dishes with the main course. A sturdy joint of roast meat requires a really tasty and filling vegetable dish as an accompaniment, so that a small amount of meat will stretch out to feed a large family. Many of these recipes are for potato-based dishes, either on their own as in the Slovene favourite, sautéed potatoes, a standard part of every Sunday lunch, or in combination with other vegetables, such as cabbage and potato hotpot. The traditional salad dish of cold mixed vegetables with sauerkraut is another Slovene favourite, and blends well with almost any main course.

There are many recipes for dumplings in Slovenia, often flavoured with herbs and spices. These tasty dumplings can be adapted to be eaten at any time of day – as a little snack with a drink or two, as additions to soup for dinner, as part of a warming stew at lunchtime or even for breakfast if there are some leftovers from the day before. They are not always savoury concoctions – the recipe for buckwheat dumplings with its sweet, cinnamon-flavoured walnut filling is ideal to serve as a substantial dessert.

Serves 6

1kg/2¼lb cabbage, shredded
500g–1kg/1¼–2¼lb potatoes, peeled
  and diced
1 onion, quartered
1 bay leaf
3 garlic cloves, chopped
5ml/1 tsp ground cumin
salt and ground black pepper
pork crackling, to serve

One-pot Cabbage and Potatoes
Govnač

Slovenia is situated on the sunny south side of the Alps, and vegetables are grown in abundance. This wintery hotpot is a typical dish of the region, which may be served on its own or as an accompaniment to roast or braised beef or garlic sausages. It is simple to make and the longer you simmer, the tastier it becomes.

1 Place the cabbage in a large pan. Add boiling water to cover and bring to the boil. Drain in a colander, then return the cabbage to the pan.

2 Add the diced potatoes, quartered onion, bay leaf, garlic and cumin to the pan, then pour in just enough fresh water or vegetable stock to cover the vegetables.

3 Slowly bring the mixture to the boil, then reduce the heat and cover the pan. Gently simmer on a low heat for 45 minutes to 1 hour, or until the vegetables are very soft.

4 Mash the vegetables into their cooking liquid. Season generously with salt and ground pepper. Serve on plates, sprinkling pork crackling over the vegetables.

COOK'S TIP
If you want the vegetable mixture to be thick, rather than have vegetables in a thick stock, use an equal weight of cabbages and potatoes.

PER SERVING: Energy 107kcal/452kJ; Protein 3.9g; Carbohydrate 22.5g, of which sugars 9.8g; Fat 0.6g, of which saturates 0.1g; Cholesterol 0mg; Calcium 89mg; Fibre 4.5g; Sodium 21mg.

Serves 6

8 to 12 potatoes
65g/2½oz/5 tbsp lard, white cooking
    fat or oil
1 onion, sliced
salt

VARIATIONS
• Cut the potatoes into cubes rather than thin slices.
• Another idea is to stir in parsley and garlic when the potatoes are crusty and brown.
• Once the sautéed potatoes are brown, you can add cooked peas and mushrooms with some extra butter, and simmer for another 3–4 minutes.
• You can also add honey, cinnamon and cloves at the end of the cooking process and then toss well to create a sweet flavour.

Sautéed Potatoes
Pražen krompir

These fried potatoes are popular for everyday eating as well as festive meals. They have been prepared all over Slovenia since the 19th century when potatoes grew in abundance and popularity. Together with beef broth and braised beef, sautéed potatoes are part of a typical Sunday family meal and can even be a stand-alone dish.

1 Peel the potatoes, or scrub the skins well and leave on for a fuller flavour – the nutty taste of the skins adds much to this dish. Put them in a large pan of boiling water and cook for about 15 minutes, until they are barely tender, then drain well.

2 Leave the potatoes until they are cool enough to handle, then cut into thin slices, about 3mm/⅛in thick.

3 While the potatoes are cooking, heat the lard in a large frying pan and add the slices of onion.

4 Gently fry the onion slices for about 10 minutes, until softened, stirring them occasionally.

5 Add the potatoes to the pan and sprinkle lightly with salt. Stir well to coat each piece of potato in the fat, then spread the slices out evenly and cover the pan.

6 Cook gently for about 20 minutes, or until the potatoes are browned and crisp underneath, and tender when you bite into them. Serve with braised beef or another meat dish.

PER SERVING: Energy 226kcal/950kJ; Protein 3.5g; Carbohydrate 33g, of which sugars 3.2g; Fat 9.8g, of which saturates 1.3g; Cholesterol 0mg; Calcium 15mg; Fibre 2.1g; Sodium 22mg.

Wild Asparagus Omelette
Fritaja s špargo

A fritaja (omelette) is a great impromptu meal that can be quickly prepared from a few simple ingredients. It is a very popular dish in the Mediterranean regions of Slovenia, where an infinite number of different fillings has been created, including smoked ham, spicy sausages, wild mushrooms and herbs, to name but a few. The beautiful colour and wonderful texture of this dish make it an impressive choice for a luncheon menu.

Serves 1

115g/4oz wild asparagus
10ml/2 tsp olive oil
2 large (US extra large) eggs
15ml/1 tbsp chopped fresh dill
15g/½oz/1 tbsp butter,
    preferably unsalted
a little smoked ham or cooked
    pancetta, diced
salt and ground black pepper

VARIATION
For a wild mushroom omelette, leave out the asparagus and cook 50g/2oz sliced wild mushrooms and 1 crushed garlic clove in the oil for 3–4 minutes. Transfer the mushrooms into a bowl and set aside. Wipe the pan clean and cook the omelette as before, then sprinkle the mushrooms down the middle, fold and serve.

COOK'S TIP
For best results, it is worth investing in an omelette pan, which has sides that make it easy to flip the fritaja smoothly with a metal spatula, without fear of breaking or tearing.

1 Cut the asparagus into small pieces, about 2cm/¾in long, discarding the tough stalk ends. Heat the olive oil in an 18cm/7in omelette pan or, alternatively, a non-stick frying pan.

2 Add the asparagus and 15ml/1 tbsp water and cook gently, stirring occasionally, until the asparagus is tender and juicy and there is still a little liquid left in the pan.

3 Meanwhile, crack the eggs into a bowl, then add the dill and salt and pepper to taste. Beat together until these are just mixed – take care not to overbeat, as this may spoil the texture of the omelette.

4 Add the butter to the pan and turn up the heat a little. When the butter is sizzling, pour in the egg and herb mixture. Cook for about 1 minute, stirring gently with a wooden spoon. When the omelette is holding together, stop stirring and leave the eggs to set.

5 Cook for a further 30 seconds or until the underside is golden brown. The top surface should be just setting. Sprinkle with a little diced smoked ham or pancetta down the middle of the omelette.

6 Using a metal spatula, fold the outside third of the omelette over the smoked ham, then fold the opposite side over that. Slide the folded omelette on to a warmed plate and serve straightaway, while it is still hot.

7 This dish is mouthwatering served with an accompaniment of fresh, hot crusty bread and a dipping plate of olive oil sprinkled with herbs, ground black pepper and sea salt. A fine chilled rosé wine will also complement and enhance the subtle flavours of the dish.

PER SERVING: Energy 341kcal/1411kJ; Protein 15.9g; Carbohydrate 2.4g, of which sugars 2.3g; Fat 30.1g, of which saturates 11.9g; Cholesterol 413mg; Calcium 91mg; Fibre 2g; Sodium 232mg.

Buckwheat Polenta with Celeriac

Ajdova polenta s šelinko

The recipe for this traditional dish from Carst has been passed down through many generations of Slovenes. Buckwheat polenta is cooled and sliced, then served with a smoked meat – such as pork, spicy salami or pancetta – and celeriac sauce, all of which complement the nutty, earthy flavour of the buckwheat to perfection.

Serves 6

Buckwheat polenta
about 2 litres/3½ pints/8¾ cups water
500g/1¼lb/4½ cups buckwheat flour
50g/2oz/½ cup plain (all-purpose) flour
15ml/1 tbsp olive oil, butter, lard or white cooking fat

Celeriac sauce
30ml/2 tbsp olive oil
1 large celeriac with leaves (if possible), about 500g/1¼lb, diced and leaves finely shredded
225g/8oz smoked pork, ham, pancetta or salami, in one piece
1 garlic clove, chopped
15ml/1 tbsp sugar
15–30ml/1–2 tbsp plain (all-purpose) flour
bunch of fresh parsley, trimmed and chopped
salt and ground black pepper

COOK'S TIP
Some cooks add 1–2 diced potatoes to the celery sauce to thicken it, and some sprinkle a few toasted pine kernels over the polenta and sauce before serving.

1 Bring the water and a pinch of salt to the boil in a large pan. Sprinkle in a handful of buckwheat flour and stir. Mix in the remaining buckwheat and plain flour, stirring thoroughly and making sure that the water bubbles all the time.

2 Cook the polenta over a high heat, stirring constantly, for about 40 minutes, until it is very thick and smooth, and comes away from the sides of the pan.

3 Add the olive oil, butter or fat and stir well. Turn the polenta out on to a board and spread it evenly to about 2cm/¾in thick, then leave to cool.

4 Meanwhile make the celeriac sauce. Heat the oil in a pan and add the diced celeriac, with the leaves. Fry, stirring all the while, for about 5 minutes, until the leaves have wilted and the celeriac is coated in the oil.

5 Add the piece of meat, garlic and sugar, then pour in just enough cold water to cover the ingredients. Bring to the boil, then cover the pan, reduce the heat and simmer for about 20 minutes, or until the celeriac is soft.

6 Preheat the oven to 180°C/350°F/Gas 4. Cut the polenta into squares or fingers and arrange them in an ovenproof dish or on a baking tray. Cover with foil and reheat in the oven for 10 minutes.

7 Remove the meat from the celeriac and dice. Blend the flour with a little cold water to make a smooth paste, then stir it into the sauce and bring it to the boil, stirring all the time.

8 Return the meat to the sauce, add the chopped parsley and simmer for 2–3 minutes, until thickened. Season to taste with salt and a twist of ground black pepper. Serve the sauce ladled over the polenta.

PER SERVING: Energy 447kcal/1872kJ; Protein 13.7g; Carbohydrate 78.9g, of which sugars 3.9g; Fat 7.7g, of which saturates 1.1g; Cholesterol 22mg; Calcium 73mg; Fibre 2.9g; Sodium 505mg.

Serves 4–6
250g/9oz cabbage
40g/1½oz/3 tbsp lard, white cooking fat
   or butter
15ml/1 tbsp sugar
1 onion, chopped
50g/2oz rindless smoked bacon, diced
pinch of ground cumin
few drops of red wine
salt

Noodle dough
200g/7oz/1¾ cups plain
   (all-purpose) flour
2 eggs
30ml/2 tbsp water

COOK'S TIP
Noodle dough can be made 1 day ahead
and chilled, wrapped in clear film (plastic
wrap). Bring to room temperature before
rolling out.

Cabbage with Noodle Squares
Zeljove krpice

A vegetable and noodle dish from Prekmurje, in north-
eastern Slovenia, this dish is enjoyed particularly during
late summer and early autumn, when fresh cabbages are
plentiful. The noodle squares are simple to make.

1 To prepare the noodles, sift the
flour into a bowl and make a well.
Add the eggs and water, then whisk
lightly with a fork. Work in the flour to
make a dough. Knead until smooth.

2 Roll out the dough thinly on a
lightly floured surface and cut into
strips about 1–2cm/½–¾in wide, then
cut them across into squares. Cut the
cabbage leaves into squares about
the same size. Set aside.

3 Boil a large pan of salted water and
add the noodle squares. Boil, reduce
the heat and simmer for 10 minutes,
until the noodles are tender.

4 Melt the lard, fat or butter in a large
pan. Add the sugar and cook until it
starts to colour. Add the onion and
bacon and cook until lightly browned.

5 Add the cabbage, cumin and salt.
Add a spoonful of cooking water from
the noodles and cook the cabbage for
3–5 minutes. Add a few drops of red
wine, mix and cook for 3 minutes.
Drain the noodle squares and mix in.

PER SERVING: Energy 230kcal/968kJ; Protein 7.4g; Carbohydrate 31.4g, of which sugars 5.8g; Fat 9.3g, of which saturates 4.6g; Cholesterol 82mg; Calcium 82mg; Fibre 2.1g; Sodium 197mg.

Serves 6
1 red cabbage, about 1kg/2¼lb,
    finely shredded
2 fairly large cooking apples, grated
5ml/1 tsp ground cumin
juice of 1 lemon
50g/2oz/¼ cup butter
45ml/3 tbsp soft brown sugar
1 onion, sliced
30ml/2 tbsp red wine vinegar or
    cider vinegar
50ml/2fl oz/¼ cup water
120ml/4fl oz/½ cup red wine
30ml/2 tbsp cranberries, chopped
salt and ground black pepper

Braised Red Cabbage
Dušeno rdeče zelje

Slovenes are very proud of their wine-making traditions. According to legend, St Martin
transformed unfermented grape juice, called must, into wine. This braised red cabbage
dish contains a generous amount of red wine and forms a classic accompaniment to
St Martin's Goose, but is equally good served with other game birds or roasted pork.

1 Place the cabbage in a large bowl.
Mix in the grated apples, cumin, lemon
juice and salt and pepper. Mix the
ingredients thoroughly, then cover and
set aside to marinate for at least 2 hours.

2 Melt the butter in a large pan. Add
the sugar and cook for a few seconds.
Stir in the onion and cook, stirring
frequently, until it is soft and just
beginning to colour. Stir in a few drops
of wine vinegar or cider vinegar and
add the cabbage mixture.

3 Pour in the water and half of the
wine and heat, stirring, until the
mixture begins to simmer. Cover
and cook gently for 30 minutes,
stirring occasionally.

4 Add the remaining wine and the
chopped cranberries and mix well,
then bring the pan back to simmering
point, reducing the heat if necessary,
and cover the pan. Cook gently for
30–40 minutes, until the cabbage is
tender, glazed and full-flavoured. Stir
occasionally during cooking. Taste for
seasoning before serving.

PER SERVING: Energy 171kcal/717kJ; Protein 2.7g; Carbohydrate 21.5g, of which sugars 21.1g; Fat 7.3g, of which saturates 4.3g; Cholesterol 18mg; Calcium 93mg; Fibre 4.4g; Sodium 65mg.

Serves 4

½ short loaf of French bread
250ml/8fl oz/1 cup milk
5 eggs, hard-boiled
3 eggs, separated
30ml/2 tbsp butter, softened, plus
　extra for greasing
5ml/1 tsp salt
15ml/1 tbsp chopped fresh marjoram
　or basil
grated rind of 1 lemon
30ml/2 tbsp sour cream
15–20g/½–¾oz dried morels,
　boiled, drained and sliced
30ml/2 tbsp chopped fresh parsley
15ml/1 tbsp dry white wine
25g/1oz asparagus tips (optional)

Ljubljana Egg Dish
Ljubljanska jajčna jed

This recipe was featured in the first Slovene cookbook by Magdalena Pleiweis, published in 1868. It is a combination of milk-soaked bread, hard-boiled eggs and morel mushrooms in a lemon and herb-flavoured custard.

1 Preheat the oven to 180ºC/350ºF/ Gas 4. Grease a soufflé dish with butter. Break the French bread into pieces and put in a bowl. Pour over the milk and set aside until softened.

2 Shell the boiled eggs. Separate the yolks and press them through a sieve (strainer). Slice the whites into strips.

3 Squeeze the milk from the bread and add half the bread to the yolks with half the butter. Mix, then stir in the raw yolks. Whisk the whites until stiff and fold into the yolk mixture. Add a pinch of salt, the marjoram or basil, lemon rind, sour cream and the remaining bread. Mix thoroughly.

4 Fry the cooked morels in the rest of the butter for 2 minutes. Add the parsley, white wine and asparagus.

5 Spread a third of the egg mixture in the dish. Sprinkle with half the morels and egg whites. Repeat and top with the last of the yolk mixture. Bake for about 30 minutes, until the dish is browned and set.

PER SERVING: Energy 321kcal/1341kJ; Protein 17.4g; Carbohydrate 17.55g, of which sugars 4.2g; Fat 20.4g, of which saturates 8.7g; Cholesterol 405mg; Calcium 186mg; Fibre 1.05g; Sodium 864mg.

Serves 4

3 large heads of chicory, about 675g/1½ lb
6 rashers (strips) smoked streaky (fatty)
    bacon, rinds removed and
    roughly chopped
3 garlic cloves, finely chopped
150ml/¼ pint/⅔ cup vegetable stock
1 bay leaf
ground black pepper

VARIATION

Just before serving, you can flavour the
chicory, if you like, with a sprinkling of
fennel seeds or chopped fresh herbs
such as chives or dill.

Gorica Chicory
Goriški radič

Young chicory is usually served raw in salads, but more
mature chicory is generally roasted or braised, as in this
recipe, which hails from the town of Nova Gorica. This
part of Slovenia has been famous for growing chicory
from the time of the Austro-Hungarian Empire.

1 Quarter the chicory lengthways.
If it is slightly old and tough, blanch
it in boiling, lightly salted water with
a pinch or two of sugar for two
minutes to remove any bitterness,
then drain well – this won't be
necessary if the chicory is young
and tender.

2 Heat a large non-stick frying pan
and cook the bacon pieces over a
medium-high heat for 3–4 minutes
or until they begin to brown. Add
the garlic and cook briefly, then
transfer on to a plate with a slotted
spoon, leaving the fat and juices
behind in the pan.

3 Add the chicory to the pan and cook
for 3–4 minutes or until it starts to
caramelize, stirring frequently. Pour
over the stock, add the bay leaf and
then return the bacon and garlic
to the pan.

4 When the stock starts to bubble,
lower the heat and cover the pan with
a lid. Simmer for 5 minutes, remove
the lid and cook for 7–8 minutes, or
until the chicory is tender and most
of the stock has evaporated. Remove
the bay leaf, then taste and season
with pepper (you won't need salt, as
the bacon will add enough). Serve hot
with a helping of boiled potatoes.

PER SERVING: Energy 117kcal/484kJ; Protein 6.8g; Carbohydrate 6.8g, of which sugars 1.4g; Fat 8.5g, of which saturates 2.9g; Cholesterol 20mg; Calcium 40mg; Fibre 2g; Sodium 396mg.

Serves 4

450g/1lb sauerkraut
115g/4oz/1 cup diced cooked
    beetroot (beets)
2 large carrots, peeled and
    coarsely grated
115g/4oz/1 cup diced cucumber
50g/2oz/⅓ cup diced celery
225g/8oz/2 cups diced cooked potatoes
6 gherkins, very finely chopped
60ml/4 tbsp chopped fresh parsley
75ml/2½fl oz/⅓ cup light olive or
    vegetable oil
30ml/2 tbsp cider vinegar
5ml/1 tsp wholegrain mustard
salt and ground black pepper

Sauerkraut Salad

Mešana zelenjavna in zeljna solata

Simple salad dishes like this one are served in many homes and restaurants. Made with a combination of raw and cooked diced vegetables, the salad is mixed with sauerkraut and is an excellent accompaniment to fritaja (omelette), sliced cold meats, frankfurters or sausages.

1 Drain the sauerkraut in a sieve (strainer), then roughly chop it into smaller pieces. Put it in a bowl with all the grated and diced beetroot, carrots, cucumber, celery and potatoes, along with half of the chopped gherkins and half of the parsley. Gently mix together.

2 Whisk the oil, vinegar, mustard, salt and pepper together in a small jug (pitcher) or bowl with a fork, or shake together well in a screw-top jar. Drizzle the mixture over the vegetables and mix well.

3 Transfer the salad to a serving bowl or platter and serve sprinkled with the remaining gherkins and parsley.

COOK'S TIP

Cover the salad and chill for a few hours to allow the flavours to develop. Remove the salad half an hour before serving. Stored in a covered bowl, the salad will keep for 2–3 days in the refrigerator.

VARIATION

You can use kisla repa, which is salted, pickled grated turnip, instead of sauerkraut if you prefer.

PER SERVING: Energy 204kcal/844kJ; Protein 4.2g; Carbohydrate 17.4g, of which sugars 8.6g; Fat 13.4g, of which saturates 1.9g; Cholesterol 0mg; Calcium 122mg; Fibre 5.7g; Sodium 823mg.

Serves 4
225g/8oz/2 cups buckwheat flour
500ml/17fl oz/2 cups boiling salted water
15ml/1 tbsp plain (all-purpose) flour

Walnut filling
30ml/2 tbsp sour cream
1 egg, lightly beaten
2.5ml/½ tsp ground cinnamon
25g/1oz/¼ cup ground walnuts
45ml/3 tbsp fresh white breadcrumbs

For serving
60ml/4 tbsp butter
30ml/2 tbsp French breadcrumbs

Buckwheat Dumplings
Ajdovi štruklji z orehi

Walnut trees grow in abundance in Slovenia and pickled green walnuts are a speciality of the country. Mature walnuts are used in many savoury and sweet dishes, including these delicious dumplings, which are fragrantly spiced with cinnamon.

1 Mix the sour cream, egg, cinnamon and walnuts together in a bowl.

2 Put the buckwheat flour in a bowl and stir in the boiling salted water to make a dough. Allow to cool slightly, then turn it out and sprinkle with flour. Knead lightly and briefly, then roll out to about 5mm/¼in thick.

3 Spread the walnut filling over the dough and sprinkle with the breadcrumbs. Roll up the dough to enclose the filling. Cut into lengths. For each piece of roll, rinse a table napkin or dish towel in hot water and wring it out. Wrap the dumpling rolls in the cloths and tie the ends securely.

4 Bring a large pan of salted water to the boil and add the dumpling rolls. Boil for 30 minutes.

5 Melt the butter in a frying pan and add the breadcrumbs. Cook, stirring, until they are crisp and brown.

6 Unwrap the dumpling rolls and cut into thick slices. Arrange on plates and spoon over the breadcrumbs with butter from the pan, then serve.

PER SERVING: Energy 470kcal/1959kJ; Protein 8.6g; Carbohydrate 63.1g, of which sugars 1.1g; Fat 20.1g, of which saturates 9.4g; Cholesterol 75mg; Calcium 65mg; Fibre 1.9g; Sodium 254mg.

Idrija Potato Pockets
Idrijski žlikrofi

Little pockets filled with potato, idrijski žlikrofi were originally eaten by miners in the 18th century. Today, these little dumplings are served with a meat sauce, bakalca, made from mutton or rabbit. They are also popular drizzled with melted butter or topped with a blue cheese.

Serves 6

Idrija filling

50g/2oz rindless streaky (fatty) smoked
 bacon or pork crackling, diced
15ml/1 tbsp olive oil
500g/1¼lb onions, chopped
500g/1¼lb potatoes, cooked
 and mashed
5ml/1 tsp dried marjoram
60ml/4 tbsp chopped fresh chives
salt and ground black pepper
melted butter, to serve
chopped fresh chives, to garnish

Dumpling dough

300g/11oz/2¾ cups plain
 (all-purpose) flour
1 egg
5ml/1 tsp olive oil
a little milk or water

COOK'S TIP

When cooking dumplings, always use a very large pan and start with plenty of lightly salted boiling water as the dumplings will absorb some of the liquid. Tossing them in melted butter after cooking stops them from sticking together as well as flavouring them.

1 For the dough, mix the flour, egg and oil, adding just enough milk or water to make a pliable dough – it should be slightly softer than the usual noodle dough but not too sticky. Turn the dough out on to a floured surface and knead thoroughly until it is very smooth and elastic.

2 Shape the dough into a large ball, place it in the clean, lightly floured, bowl and cover with cling film (plastic wrap). Set aside to rest for 30 minutes.

3 To make the filling, cook the bacon in the oil until the fat runs, then add the onions and continue to cook, stirring frequently, until the bacon and onions are soft but not browned.

4 Stir the onion mixture into the mashed potatoes with the marjoram, chives and seasoning to taste. Shape the potato mixture into small balls about the size of hazelnuts (filberts) and set them aside on a tray.

5 Roll out the noodle dough thinly and trim the edges neatly. Lay a row of filling balls along one edge of the dough, leaving enough dough between them to fold up and enclose each ball of filling. Cut the dough into a long narrow strip that is wide enough to enclose the filling, then carefully cut between each small ball of filling.

6 Fold up the edges of each piece of dough to enclose the filling, brush with butter and then pinch the ends to seal them. The ends should look like little ears. Repeat with all of the remaining filling, balls and dough.

7 Place the filled dumplings on a lightly floured tray or plate. Each dumpling should be about 4cm/1½in long and about 2cm/¾in high.

8 Bring a large pan of salted water to the boil and cook the dumplings (in batches if necessary) until they float. Drain them and serve them hot, dressed with lashings of hot melted butter and sprinkled with chopped chives.

PER SERVING: Energy 318kcal/1343kJ; Protein 9.7g; Carbohydrate 59.1g, of which sugars 6.7g; Fat 6.4g, of which saturates 1.5g; Cholesterol 37mg; Calcium 118mg; Fibre 4g; Sodium 133mg.

Tarragon Rolled Dumpling
Pehtranovi štruklji

Štruklji are the most well-known Slovene dumplings and there are at least 70 different versions. A multi-purpose dish, they can be served alone, often with a side salad, as an accompaniment to a meat dish, or as a sweetened dessert. Their versatility and simplicity make them a popular staple dish with Slovene cooks.

Serves 6

50g/2oz/¼ cup butter
90ml/6 tbsp fresh white breadcrumbs
filo pastry (page 18), or 6 bought filo
    pastry sheets, each about
    30 x 18cm/12 x 7in
300ml/½ pint/1¼ cups thick sour cream
2 eggs, separated
2 bunches fresh tarragon, trimmed
    and chopped
salt

VARIATION

The tarragon rolled dumpling can be served as a savoury dish, as here, or it can be generously sprinkled with icing (confectioners') sugar or drizzled with honey and served as a sweet dish.

COOK'S TIPS

• The dumpling can be wrapped in foil instead of using a scalded dish towel. Brush the foil with a little oil and fold over the edges, then twist the ends. If the foil is thin, use a double thickness.
• If you do not have a large enough pan to simmer the dumpling, cut the dough into two pieces and wrap each separately.

1 Melt half of the butter in a pan and add half of the breadcrumbs. Cook, stirring, until the crumbs are lightly browned. Remove from the heat and set aside to cool.

2 Prepare, roll and cut the pastry following the recipe instructions. If you are using bought pastry, lay three sheets of filo pastry on a lightly floured surface, overlapping their short edges well so that they form an oblong that measures about 18 x 70cm/7 x 27in. The long side of the oblong should be nearest you. Top with the remaining three sheets to give a large double-thick pastry base.

3 Mix the sour cream, egg yolks, fried breadcrumbs and tarragon. In a perfectly clean bowl, whisk the egg whites until they are quite stiff, then fold them into the tarragon mixture.

4 Spread this filling thinly over the pastry, leaving a 2.5cm/1in margin around the edges, then roll up both pastry and filling from the long side.

5 Scald a dish towel in boiling water, wring out and wrap this around the dumpling roll. Tie the ends with string. Bring a large pan, such as a fish poaching pan, of salted water to the boil. Lower the dumpling into the water and bring back to simmering point. Cover the pan and simmer steadily for about 25 minutes or so.

6 Meanwhile, melt the remaining butter in a pan and fry the remaining breadcrumbs until they are golden in colour.

7 Carefully lift the dumpling from the pan and unwrap it, then slice the cooked dumpling into pieces. Serve the dish sprinkled with the buttery breadcrumbs, and accompanied by your favourite vegetable dish, such as braised red cabbage (page 61) or mixed vegetable and sauerkraut salad (page 64).

PER SERVING: Energy 367kcal/1540kJ; Protein 11.9g; Carbohydrate 43.2g, of which sugars 3.2g; Fat 17.6g, of which saturates 7g; Cholesterol 134mg; Calcium 115mg; Fibre 1.8g; Sodium 306mg.

MEAT DISHES

Baked Meatballs

Beef in Horseradish Sauce

Smoked Ham Meatloaf

Roast Lamb

Visoko Stuffed Loin of Pork

Slovene Pork Sausages

Tripe Stew

St Martin's Goose with Mlinci

Chicken Casserole

Tender pork to moist meatballs

Every country in Europe has its own traditions for making the most of small amounts of meat. In Slovenia, small-scale farms relied on the family pig to feed them throughout the cold winter. Nothing could be wasted, hence the delicious sausages made from the lesser cuts of meat and smoked or air-dried with herbs and spices. These would last for several months and then form the basis of many stews and soups. Beef is another Slovene favourite, especially for Sunday lunch, when a beef broth might serve as the appetizer, followed by braised beef as the main course, with sautéed potatoes, naturally. Poultry such as turkey, goose and chicken were also raised on Slovene farms and would be eaten for a treat or on feast days such as St Martin's Day.

In the interest of using every part of the animal, many Slovenes enjoy eating tripe (the lining of an animal's stomach, usually an ox). The recipe given here uses ready-cooked tripe and adds a spicy sauce and plenty of garlic. It is an acquired taste – but definitely worth a try as a nutritious snack or side dish.

Serves 6
500g/1¼lb lightly cooked pork and offal
    (brains and lungs)
50g/2oz/¼ cup lard or 60ml/4 tbsp
    vegetable oil
1 large onion, chopped
1 garlic clove, crushed
pinch of ground cinnamon
1.5 litres/2½ pints/6¼ cups stock or water
1 bay leaf
350g/12oz/3 cups instant polenta
1 egg, beaten
caul fat
salt and ground black pepper

VARIATION
To use a traditional pig's head for this
dish, ask a butcher to chop one into
pieces. Wash thoroughly, boil and simmer
for 1 minute. Drain, cover with fresh
water, then add onion and fresh herbs.
Boil and simmer for about 2 hours.

Baked Meatballs
Mavžlji

These are a much-loved delicacy in Alpine regions.
They combine meat with offal, cooked in a wrapping
of caul fat. Serve them piping hot from the oven with
potatoes and braised sauerkraut or sour turnip.

1 Lightly season the meat and offal
with salt and pepper, then mince
(grind) it or finely chop.

2 Heat the lard in a pan, add the
onion and cook for 10 minutes until
soft. Add the garlic and cinnamon.

3 While the onion is cooking, bring
the stock, bay leaf and a pinch of salt
to the boil. Add the polenta in a
stream, stirring continuously, and
cook for 5 minutes, until the mixture
has thickened and is pulling from the
sides of the pan. Remove the bay leaf.

4 Add the onion and fat from the pan to
the polenta with the minced meat, the
beaten egg and seasoning. Mix well.

5 Preheat the oven to 180ºC/350ºF/
Gas 4. Wetting your hands, shape the
mixture into small fist-size balls.
Wrap each in a piece of caul fat and
put in a roasting pan, in a single layer.

6 Bake the meatballs for 1 hour or
until well browned and the caul fat
has melted. Serve immediately.

PER SERVING: Energy 428kcal/1786kJ; Protein 30.4g; Carbohydrate 42.6g, of which sugars 0g; Fat 14.4g, of which saturates 4.1g; Cholesterol 39mg; Calcium 10mg; Fibre 1.3g; Sodium 102mg.

Serves 4–6
500g–1kg/1¼–2¼lb cooked beef
15ml/1 tbsp plain (all-purpose) flour
1 ladleful cold beef soup or stock
200ml/7fl oz/scant 1 cup sour cream
15ml/1 tbsp wine vinegar
30ml/2 tbsp grated horseradish
1–2 egg yolks
30–45ml/2–3 tbsp grated
   Parmesan cheese
salt and ground black pepper

Beef in Horseradish Sauce
Govedina v hrenovi omaki

This dish demonstrates the creativeness of Slovene cooks. Here, left-over beef is transformed into a delicious dinner with a rich and creamy sauce. Sautéed potatoes or noodles and a green vegetable, such as beans or steamed shredded cabbage, would make a perfect accompaniment for this meal.

1 Preheat the oven to 150°C/300°F/ Gas 2. Slice the beef. Fold the slices neatly and arrange them in a shallow ovenproof dish.

2 For the sauce, place the flour in a pan and stir in the cold soup or stock to make a smooth paste. Then stir in the sour cream, wine vinegar, grated horseradish, and salt and pepper. Bring to the boil, stirring continuously, remove from the heat and set aside to cool for 15 minutes.

3 Stir a few spoonfuls of the warm sauce into the egg yolks until well mixed, then pour the mixture into the main batch of sauce. Mix thoroughly, then pour the sauce over the meat to coat it evenly. Sprinkle with Parmesan. Bake for 30 minutes, until the top is lightly browned and the beef is hot.

VARIATION
Horseradish vapours are very pungent when grating. If you prefer, use 30ml/ 2 tbsp hot horseradish sauce. Creamed horseradish sauce can also be used.

PER SERVING: Energy 257kcal/1070kJ; Protein 22.6g; Carbohydrate 3.6g, of which sugars 1.7g; Fat 17g, of which saturates 8.6g; Cholesterol 107mg; Calcium 104mg; Fibre 0.2g; Sodium 124mg.

Smoked Ham Meatloaf
Gorenjska prata

The addition of milk-soaked bread makes this meatloaf really moist and makes a little meat go a long way. Prata is a festive dish, usually enjoyed at Easter. In this version from Gorenjska, in northern Slovenia, the meat mixture is wrapped in lacy caul fat to hold the loaf together and to keep in the delicious juices. Serve it with horseradish sauce and root vegetables, such as carrots, parsnips and turnips, roasted in the oven at the same time.

Serves 6

500g/1¼lb smoked gammon (smoked ham) in one piece
400g/14oz dry white bread
225ml/7½fl oz/scant 1 cup milk
50ml/2fl oz/¼ cup sour cream
2 eggs, lightly beaten
30ml/2 tbsp olive oil, lard or white cooking fat, plus extra for cooking
1 onion, chopped
2 garlic cloves, chopped
60ml/4 tbsp chopped fresh parsley
freshly grated nutmeg
1 piece of pork caul, thoroughly rinsed and drained
ground black pepper

COOK'S TIP
Instead of using caul fat, the meatloaf may be baked in a lined and buttered 1.75 litre/3 pint/7 cup loaf tin (pan), loosely covered with foil. Remove the foil for the last 15 minutes of cooking time to allow the loaf to brown a little.

1 Soak the gammon for several hours in plenty of cold water. Transfer to a pan and pour in enough fresh cold water to cover it. Bring to the boil, reduce the heat, cover and simmer for 30 minutes. Remove the gammon and when it is cool enough to handle, remove the rind (but not the fat).

2 Cut the bread into cubes and place them in a large bowl. Pour in the milk and sour cream, then add the eggs and stir well. Set the bread aside to soften while you are preparing the meat.

3 Cut the meat and its fat into chunks and mince (grind) or finely chop in a food processor or by hand. Add the meat to the bread mixture.

4 Preheat the oven to 180°C/350°F/Gas 4. Heat the oil or fat in a pan. Add the onion and cook, stirring, for 5 minutes until softened. Add the garlic, parsley, pepper and a generous sprinkling of grated nutmeg to the mixture. (There's no need to add salt as the gammon will be salty enough already.) Stir the ingredients well until they are thoroughly combined.

5 Mould the mixture into a loaf shape. Lay the caul fat on a board and place the loaf in the middle, then wrap it around the mixture to enclose it completely.

6 Place the meatloaf in a small loaf tin (pan) and drizzle a little oil over it or dot it with lard. Roast the meatloaf for about 1 hour, until it is well browned and cooked through, basting it once or twice during cooking.

7 When the meatloaf is ready, remove it from the oven, cover loosely with foil and leave to stand for 10 minutes. Serve cut into thick slices.

PER SERVING: Energy 401kcal/1690kJ; Protein 25g; Carbohydrate 43.5g, of which sugars 4.3g; Fat 15.5g, of which saturates 4.7g; Cholesterol 89mg; Calcium 159mg; Fibre 1.8g; Sodium 1208mg.

Serves 4–6
olive oil, for greasing
2 large fresh rosemary sprigs
1kg/2¼lb rack of lamb
about 50ml/2fl oz/¼ cup water
30ml/2 tbsp plain (all-purpose) flour
30ml/2 tbsp sour cream
salt and ground black pepper

Roast Lamb
Pečeno jagnje

Slovenes love to eat in the open air. In the south-eastern Slovene region of Bela Krajina, you'll see lamb being roasted on outdoor spits. Roast lamb is also a favourite dish for family celebrations. This is a typical recipe, fragrant with rosemary and served with cooking juices that have been enriched with tangy sour cream.

1 Preheat the oven to 190°C/375°F/ Gas 5. Lightly grease a roasting pan with olive oil. Chop the rosemary leaves finely, and rub the rosemary, salt and pepper all over the lamb. Place in the pan and pour in water, adding enough to cover the bottom.

2 Roast the lamb for about 1 hour, or until cooked to your liking. During the roasting process, baste the meat occasionally.

3 Transfer the lamb to a warmed dish, cover loosely with foil and set aside. Strain the cooking juices and return them to the pan.

4 Blend the flour to a smooth paste with a little cold water and stir this into the juices. Boil the mixture, scraping any residue off the pan. Simmer, stirring, for 2–3 minutes, then stir in the sour cream and remove from the heat. Season to taste.

5 Carve the lamb into separate cutlets and serve them moistened with sauce. Offer the diners roast new potatoes and buttered new carrots with the lamb.

PER SERVING: Energy 499kcal/2073kJ; Protein 29.5g; Carbohydrate 4.1g, of which sugars 0.3g; Fat 40.7g, of which saturates 19.8g; Cholesterol 128mg; Calcium 32mg; Fibre 0.2g; Sodium 104mg.

Serves 6

2 carrots
1.5kg/3¼lb boneless loin of pork
pinch of ground cumin
6 cloves
1 lemon, cut into 12 thin wedges
2 garlic cloves, finely sliced
leaves from a bunch of fresh parsley
1 large bay leaf, quartered
lard, white cooking fat or vegetable oil
    for frying
salt and ground black pepper

COOK'S TIPS

• Save some of the crackling to make
crackling flat cakes (see page 26).
• Any pieces of left-over pork can be
thinly sliced and served cold with a salad
such as sauerkraut salad (see page 64).

Visoko Stuffed Loin of Pork
Visoška pečenka

Roasts make a great Sunday lunch because they need
little attention once they are in the oven. Served with
roast potatoes and braised red cabbage, roast pork
stuffed with carrots is a traditional family dish on Palm
Sunday. This recipe is from the Poljanska valley.

1 Preheat the oven to 220°C/425°F/
Gas 7. Cut the carrots lengthways
into three, and simmer in salted
water for 7–8 minutes, until tender.

2 Lay the pork skin side up, and use
a sharp knife to score the rind
crossways. Turn the meat over and
make a 1cm/½in deep cut along its
length. Season the meat well with
salt and pepper and sprinkle with a
little cumin. Press the carrots into
the slit along the piece of meat.

3 Stick cloves in the meat and cover
with lemon wedges, garlic and
parsley leaves. Add pieces of bay leaf.

4 Fold the sides of the meat up to
form a neat roll and then tie it up
evenly with a piece of strong string.
Place the meat in a roasting pan and
then rub the skin liberally with salt
to add flavour.

5 Roast the joint for about
30 minutes, then reduce the oven
temperature to 190°C/375°F/Gas 5
and cook for an additional 1½ hours,
or until the meat is tender and
cooked through.

6 Cover the meat with foil and leave
to stand in a warm place for
10 minutes before carving.

PER SERVING: Energy 393kcal/1643kJ; Protein 53.6g; Carbohydrate 1.3g, of which sugars 1.2g; Fat 19.2g, of which saturates 4.5g; Cholesterol 158mg; Calcium 22mg; Fibre 0.4g; Sodium 179mg.

Makes about 1kg/2¼lb
sausage casings
3 garlic cloves
50ml/2fl oz/¼ cup water
600g/1lb 5oz lean boneless pork
400g/14oz rindless streaky (fatty) bacon
15ml/1 tbsp salt
1.8ml/⅓ tsp peppercorns, crushed

Slovene Pork Sausages
Kranjska klobasa

Slovenia is known for its fabulous semi-dried lightly smoked sausages that are still made
to centuries-old recipes. This recipe is for simpler fresh unsmoked sausages, but like
traditional versions, still contains generous amounts of crushed peppercorns and garlic.

1 Soak the sausage casings in cold
water for 1 hour. Drain and rinse the
casings several times, then place in
cold water until needed. Crush the
garlic into a small bowl and add water.
Stir and infuse (steep) for 10 minutes.

2 Finely mince (grind) the meat and
bacon (this would traditionally have
been done with a knife). Place in a bowl
and add salt and pepper. Strain the
garlic water over the meat (discard
the garlic) and mix thoroughly by hand.

3 Use a nylon piping (pastry) bag with
a large nozzle to fill the sausage skins.
Put some meat mixture into the bag.
Drain a piece of skin and push on to the
nozzle, sliding it up and wrinkling it
back firmly. Tie a knot in the other end;
gently squeeze in the meat until packed.

4 When the sausage casing is full, tie
the end firmly. Knot the other end and
twist the sausage into even links.

5 To cook, gently fry in a little oil for
12–15 minutes, over a low heat, turning
until browned and cooked through.
Serve with horseradish or mustard.

TOTAL MIXTURE: Energy 1865kcal/7763kJ; Protein 194g; Carbohydrate 4.9g, of which sugars 0.5g; Fat 118.6g, of which saturates 41.2g; Cholesterol 638mg; Calcium 73mg; Fibre 1.2g; Sodium 11356mg.

Serves 6

60ml/4 tbsp vegetable or olive oil
50g/2oz rindless bacon, diced
2 onions, finely chopped
1 bay leaf
400g/14oz prepared tripe, sliced
5ml/1 tsp paprika
30ml/2 tbsp tomato purée (paste)
25g/1oz/½ cup fresh white breadcrumbs
45ml/3 tbsp white wine
45ml/3 tbsp water
4 garlic cloves, finely chopped
fresh flat leaf parsley
salt and ground black pepper
Parmesan cheese or other hard cheese,
    grated, to serve

Tripe Stew
Vampi

Tripe is a speciality of all regions surrounding the Adriatic and is a particular favourite of Ljubljana. This recipe is popular as a mid-morning snack or for lunch. It is often added to goulash and washed down with a mug or two of local beer.

1 Heat the oil in a large pan. Add the bacon and cook for 2–3 minutes, then add the onions and bay leaf, and cook, stirring occasionally, over a low heat, for 15–20 minutes, until the onions are very tender.

2 Add the tripe, paprika, tomato purée and white breadcrumbs. Stir in the wine and water and lightly season with salt. Bring to the boil, stirring, and gently simmer for 2–3 minutes.

3 Stir in the garlic and add a sprinkling of fresh parsley leaves. Taste for seasoning and serve. You can add grated Parmesan or other hard cheese as an accompaniment.

COOK'S TIP
Tripe is available from many butchers and supermarkets. When purchasing, check that the tripe has already been cooked and not just blanched. If it hasn't been pre-cooked, you will need to simmer it in step 2 for an additional 15 minutes, or until it is really tender.

PER SERVING: Energy 166kcal/691kJ; Protein 8.2g; Carbohydrate 11.4g, of which sugars 5.5g; Fat 9.6g, of which saturates 1.5g; Cholesterol 47mg; Calcium 69mg; Fibre 1.4g; Sodium 209mg.

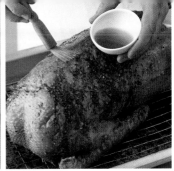

St Martin's Goose with Mlinci

Martinova gos z mlinci

St Martin is the patron saint of grapevines and wines, and in his honour there are great celebrations in mid-November – according to legend, this is when the saint turned unfermented grape juice (must) into wine. Stories tell that when he was elected as bishop, he hid among geese who gave him away, so as 'punishment' a goose (and occasionally an unfortunate duck) is served as the classic centrepiece for this meal.

Serves 6

50g/2oz/¼ cup butter
6 shallots, peeled
1 goose
good pinch of dried marjoram
pinch of ground cumin
5 small eating apples, peeled and cored
200–250g/7–8oz peeled
 cooked chestnuts
120ml/4fl oz/½ cup dry white wine
50ml/2fl oz/¼ cup fruit spirit (liqueur),
 such as tropinovec
salt and ground black pepper

To serve

Braised Red Cabbage (see page 61)
Mlinci (see page 19)

COOK'S TIP

Tropinovec is distilled from fermented grapes that are left over from wine production ('tropine' means half-dried grapes) and blended with sugar. It is usually mixed with fruits such as cherries or pears. If you can't find it on sale, a fruit liqueur such as cherry brandy makes a good substitute in this recipe.

1 Preheat the oven to 180°C/350°F/Gas 4. Melt the butter in a small pan, add the shallots and cook, stirring continuously, for about 5 minutes, until they are beginning to brown. Remove from the heat.

2 Weigh the goose and calculate the cooking time at 40 minutes per 1kg/2¼lb, plus 30 minutes (or 20 minutes per pound, plus 30 minutes). Prick the skin of the goose all over with a fork and season the bird generously, both inside and out, then sprinkle the marjoram and cumin inside.

3 Stuff the goose with the whole apples, chestnuts and shallots. Sew up the flap over the neck end of the bird (or secure with small metal skewers).

4 Place the goose in a large roasting pan, add the wine and roast the goose slowly, turning it twice and basting it with the cooking juices. The goose must be evenly roasted from every side.

5 Remove any excess fat from the pan occasionally during cooking, spooning it off the cooking juices before disturbing them by turning or basting the bird.

6 About 15 minutes before the end of the cooking time, with the breast up, brush the fruit spirit or brandy over the goose. This will give the skin a golden glaze and crisp texture.

7 Remove the bird from the oven and cover it with foil, then leave it to stand for 15 minutes before serving with red cabbage and mlinci.

8 Pour the fat and juices from the pan into a gravy jug (pitcher), leaving 15ml/ 1 tbsp fat behind in the pan. Stir 15ml/1 tbsp flour into the pan. Pour in the stock, leaving any fat in the jug. Simmer for 2–3 minutes until thickened.

PER SERVING: Energy 607kcal/2517kJ; Protein 22.5g; Carbohydrate 10.1g, of which sugars 9.7g; Fat 50.6g, of which saturates 17.2g; Cholesterol 126mg; Calcium 20mg; Fibre 1.3g; Sodium 148mg.

Chicken Casserole
Piščančja obara

Flavoured with fragrant fresh herbs, lemon juice and white wine, this chicken casserole makes a great light meal for any occasion. Serve with polenta (see page 58) or boiled new potatoes to soak up some of the delicious gravy.

Serves 6

75g/3oz/6 tbsp butter, preferably unsalted
1 large chicken, cut into portions
1 onion, chopped
40g/1½oz/⅓ cup plain (all-purpose) flour
250ml/8fl oz/1 cup dry white wine
about 1 litre/1¾ pints/4 cups chicken or vegetable stock
2 carrots, peeled and cut into large chunks
1 garlic clove, peeled
bunch of fresh parsley
1 fresh thyme sprig
1 fresh marjoram sprig
grated rind and juice of 1 lemon
½ cauliflower, broken into florets
115g/4oz/1 cup peas
vinegar (optional)
salt and ground black pepper

COOK'S TIP

If you would like to make a lower-fat dish, reduce the amount of butter to 40g/½oz/3 tbsp and remove the skin from the chicken before you pan-fry it.

1 Melt the butter in a large flameproof casserole dish or stockpot. Brown the chicken pieces all over, removing them from the pan when they are browned and setting them aside in a bowl.

2 Add the onion to the buttery pan juices and cook, stirring, for 3–4 minutes until the onion is softened slightly. Next, stir in the flour and cook, stirring all the time, until it is lightly browned.

3 Season with salt and pepper, then gradually blend in the wine and stock. Cook, stirring for a minute, and bring to the boil, stirring all the time until it is blended and smooth.

4 Add the carrots and the garlic clove. Tie the parsley, thyme and marjoram together and add to the casserole with the lemon rind and half the juice. Add the browned chicken portions with any juices from the bowl.

5 Slowly bring to the boil, then reduce the heat so that it simmers gently – check that all the chicken portions are covered with liquid. Rearrange the portions or add a little extra stock if necessary.

6 Cover and simmer over a medium heat for about 1 hour, or until the chicken portions and vegetables are both tender.

7 Add the cauliflower and peas halfway through the cooking, distributing them evenly over the top of the other ingredients. Bring the liquid back to a steady simmer before continuing to time the cooking.

8 Taste the dish for seasoning, adding salt and a few twists of ground black pepper. To boost the tanginess, add the remaining lemon juice before serving. A little splash of vinegar may also be added to further sharpen the flavour of the casserole.

PER SERVING: Energy 537kcal/2227kJ; Protein 34.3g; Carbohydrate 11g, of which sugars 3.6g; Fat 36.8g, of which saturates 14.4g; Cholesterol 189mg; Calcium 47mg; Fibre 2.4g; Sodium 229mg.

FISH DISHES

Polenta with Creamed Stockfish

Cuttlefish with Swiss Chard

Soča Trout with Prosciutto

Mussels in White Wine Sauce

Stuffed Squid

Piran Baked Fish

Marinated Fish

Baked Pike in Sour Cream

Fish Goulash

Oven-roasted Carp

Scrumptious squid to tasty mussels

All kinds of fish and shellfish are eaten in Slovenia, despite the fact that the coastline is so short. Many of these recipes mix fish with other ingredients, or use a marinade to make sure that the fish is tenderized to perfection.

    The country's bountiful lakes and rivers yield a splendid harvest of freshwater fish. Trout is a great favourite, gently cooked with garlic and white wine to preserve its fresh taste. Both carp and pike blend beautifully with local ingredients, such as earthy mushrooms, smoked bacon and ham, onions and herbs. On the coast, the little port of Piran has lent its name to a tasty dish of white fish with chopped vegetables and – the secret ingredient – raisins soaked in lemon juice. The fish is simply covered in the raisins and vegetables and baked in the oven until beautifully cooked through.

    On fishing boats, cod from the cold north was traditionally preserved in salt for the long journey home to southern Europe. This stiff, salty fish is cooked in a creamy sauce and served with polenta to absorb the rich flavours.

Polenta with Creamed Stockfish
Polenta z bakalarjem

In the Mediterranean area of Slovenia polenta was everyday fare, originally prepared in a copper kettle above the fireplace. Today, it is often partnered with stockfish, pounded with garlic and olive oil, to make a classic Christmas dish served with sauerkraut.

Serves 4
250g/9oz white stockfish
3 garlic cloves, peeled
about 475ml/16fl oz/2 cups olive oil
60ml/4 tbsp chopped fresh parsley
salt and ground black pepper

Polenta
900ml/1½ pints/3¾ cups vegetable stock
125g/4oz instant polenta
15ml/1 tbsp olive oil, lard or white cooking fat
salt

VARIATION
For a serving variation to this dish, pour out the polenta on to a board and spread it evenly, then leave it to cool and set. Cut the polenta into squares or stamp out circles with a glass. Fry the polenta in olive oil until golden, turning once, and serve with the creamed cod.

COOK'S TIP
Stockfish is an unsalted fish imported from countries with cooler climates such as Norway. The fish is usually cod, but may be other white fish such as pollack or haddock. It is sun and air-dried in the coldest months, then further dried and matured inside for an additional 3 months.

1 Thoroughly beat the stockfish to soften it. Soak the fish in plenty of cold water for at least 5 hours, or preferably overnight.

2 Drain the fish and place in a large pan. Add plenty of water and a good pinch of salt, then bring to the boil. Reduce the heat and simmer steadily for 15 minutes, until the fish softens. Drain the fish, saving about 250ml/8fl oz/ 1 cup water. Remove the bones and skin from the fish while it is still warm and put in a deep bowl.

3 While the fish is cooking, gently fry 2 garlic cloves in 200ml/7fl oz/scant 1 cup olive oil until slightly brown. Leave to cool for 15 minutes, then remove the garlic.

4 Pour the cooled oil over the fish, sprinkle with pepper and start pounding the fish with a large pestle, meat mallet or rolling pin. Chop the remaining garlic and add to the fish with the parsley. Continue pounding and beating the mixture.

5 When the fish has broken down and the olive oil is incorporated, gradually pour in more olive oil, a little at a time, beating continuously with a wooden spoon. The amount of oil required varies according to the texture of fish; the mixture should become thick and creamy, forming a purée.

6 Taste the creamed fish and add salt and pepper if necessary. You can also add a little cooking water from the fish to soften the purée.

7 For the polenta, bring the stock or water to the boil in a large pan with a pinch of salt. Remove from the heat and add the polenta, stirring constantly.

8 Return the polenta to a low heat and simmer, stirring frequently, for 5 minutes. Remove from the heat and stir in the olive oil, lard or fat. Taste and season with a little more salt, if needed, and ground pepper. Spoon the polenta on to plates and serve with the creamed fish.

PER SERVING: Energy 574kcal/2382kJ; Protein 24.2g; Carbohydrate 24.6g, of which sugars 0.3g; Fat 41.9g, of which saturates 5.8g; Cholesterol 37mg; Calcium 24mg; Fibre 1.3g; Sodium 252mg.

Serves 6
45ml/3 tbsp olive oil
1 onion, sliced
2 garlic cloves, chopped
675g/1½lb prepared cuttlefish, sliced
1.5kg/3¼lb Swiss chard or large spinach
   leaves, washed and shredded
bunch of fresh parsley, trimmed
   and chopped
30–45ml/2–3 tbsp water or light
   vegetable stock

Cuttlefish with Swiss Chard
Sipe z blitvo

Cuttlefish are usually sold pre-prepared, or the fishmonger will do this for you; if not, see the instructions below. This recipe is typical of the type of cooking found in the Mediterranean regions of Slovenia, where the dish is served with polenta.

1 Heat the olive oil in a pan. Add the onion and garlic and cook for about 15 minutes, until the onion is soft.

2 Add the cuttlefish and fry for a few minutes, stirring and turning the slices, until firm and lightly cooked. Sprinkle with chopped parsley and pour in the water or stock, just enough to cover the bottom of the pan and braise the cuttlefish without covering it. Gently simmer for 5 minutes, stirring.

3 Add the rinsed Swiss chard and season. Simmer and cook for 10 minutes, stirring until the chard is reduced and the cuttlefish is tender. The cooking juices will evaporate to leave the mixture moist but not wet. Serve.

COOK'S TIP
To clean the cuttlefish, cut off the tentacles in front of the eyes and remove the mouth. Remove the head, cut open the body from top to bottom and remove the cuttlebone and innards. Scrape the inside clean and rinse well. Remove the skin from the outside of the body and from the tentacles if they are large.

PER SERVING: Energy 196kcal/813kJ; Protein 25.2g; Carbohydrate 4.8g, of which sugars 4.3g; Fat 8.3g, of which saturates 1.3g; Cholesterol 124mg; Calcium 494mg; Fibre 5.4g; Sodium 767mg.

Serves 4–6
4–6 trout (one per person), about
    275g/10oz each, cleaned
4–6 garlic cloves, chopped
bunch of fresh flat leaf parsley, trimmed
115g/4oz/1 cup butter
4–6 slices prosciutto
250ml/8fl oz/1 cup white wine
salt and ground black pepper

Soča Trout with Prosciutto
Soška postrv s pršutom

Slovene trout from the Soca river are often smoked or cooked with simple flavourings as in this recipe, so that the delicious and delicate flavour of the fish shines through. Serve with buttery new potatoes and a chicory salad.

1 Preheat the oven to 180°C/350°F/ Gas 4. Rinse the trout in cold water and pat dry on kitchen paper. Season inside the fish with salt and pepper and tuck in the garlic and parsley.

2 Butter an ovenproof dish large enough to hold the fish in one layer. Wrap each trout in a slice of prosciutto and place in the dish.

3 Pour the wine over the fish and bake for 30–40 minutes, or until the fish is opaque and flakes easily, basting occasionally with cooking liquor.

4 Remove the fish from the dish and keep warm. Strain the cooking liquid into a small pan and boil rapidly until reduced by half. Pour over the fish and serve immediately.

COOK'S TIP
A cucumber and yogurt sauce is popular with trout. Grate ½ cucumber, put into a sieve (strainer) and press to squeeze out the juices. Mix the cucumber with 150g/5oz/ ⅔ cup plain yogurt, 30ml/2 tbsp chopped fresh mint and a little salt and pepper.

PER SERVING: Energy 323kcal/1345kJ; Protein 27g; Carbohydrate 0.4g, of which sugars 0.4g; Fat 20.8g, of which saturates 11.6g; Cholesterol 152mg; Calcium 45mg; Fibre 0g; Sodium 434mg.

Mussels in White Wine Sauce

Pedoči v omaki na belo

Small tender mussels are gathered from Slovenia's tiny coastline throughout the autumn and winter months from September to April. This recipe is the best and simplest way to serve these delicious seafood morsels. Unlike many other European mussel recipes, the cooking juices are thickened with breadcrumbs before serving.

Serves 4
2kg/4½lb mussels
45ml/3 tbsp olive oil
200ml/7fl oz/scant 1 cup white wine
2 garlic cloves, chopped
bunch of fresh parsley, trimmed
 and chopped
about 50g/2oz/1 cup fresh
 white breadcrumbs
pepper

1 Gently scrub the mussels, scraping off any barnacles and pulling out the fibrous 'beards' that are used by the creatures to cling on to rocks. Discard any open mussels that do not shut when lightly tapped.

2 Pour the olive oil and wine into a large pan. Add the garlic and parsley and season with a little pepper, but do not add salt.

3 Bring to the boil, add the mussels, then cover with a tight-fitting lid and cook over a moderate heat, shaking the pan occasionally, for 4–5 minutes, or until the mussels have all opened up.

4 Use a slotted spoon to remove the mussels (discarding any mussels that do not open) and place in a large bowl. Strain the cooking liquid through a sieve (strainer) lined with muslin (cheesecloth) and return to the rinsed-out pan.

5 Add the breadcrumbs to the cooking juices and bring to the boil, stirring. Boil for about a minute so that the breadcrumbs thicken the sauce.

COOK'S TIPS
• Check the mussels after 4 minutes; they are ready as soon as they have opened. Take care not to overcook, or they will toughen unpleasantly.
• Discard any mussels with broken shells prior to cooking and any that do not open, as they are not safe to eat.

6 Add a little more wine and/or breadcrumbs, if necessary, to give the sauce a good consistency. Boil again after adding any additional wine or crumbs.

7 Divide the mussels between warmed serving dishes. Return any juices from the bowl to the sauce and then pour it over them. Serve immediately.
This dish is delicious served with a fine white wine such as a Chenin Blanc, Pinot Blanc or Pinot Grigio.

PER SERVING: Energy 549kcal/2284kJ; Protein 27.9g; Carbohydrate 10.3g, of which sugars 0.9g; Fat 40.9g, of which saturates 5.8g; Cholesterol 60mg; Calcium 341mg; Fibre 0.9g; Sodium 416mg.

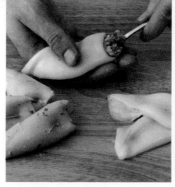

Serves 4
12 small squid with tentacles, cleaned
bunch of fresh parsley, trimmed
    and chopped
3 garlic cloves
about 50g/2oz/1 cup fresh white
    breadcrumbs
30ml/2 tbsp olive oil
about 250ml/8fl oz/1 cup white wine
salt and ground black pepper

Stuffed Squid
Polnjeni kalamari

Calamari or squid have always been popular in the Littoral area of Slovenia as well as farther inland. Larger squid need long slow cooking, but tiny tender squid are served sautéed, deep-fried, poached or grilled. They are also a popular addition to risottos.

1 Cut the squid tentacles just below the eyes, being sure not to cut the ink sac. Be sure to remove the beak at the base of the tentacles. Chop the tentacles and mix them with the parsley, garlic and breadcrumbs. Season with a little salt and pepper. There should be enough filling for the squid sacs; add more breadcrumbs if there is too little mixture.

2 Divide the mixture among the squid, but don't pack the stuffing too tightly because it will expand a little during cooking. Secure firmly with wooden cocktail sticks (toothpicks).

3 Heat the olive oil in a frying pan and fry the squid over a medium heat, turning occasionally, until the pieces are lightly browned on both sides. Pour in the white wine and bring to the boil, then reduce the heat and simmer for 15 minutes, turning the squid occasionally, until cooked through.

4 Transfer the squid to plates and serve. If there is still quite a lot of liquid left, boil it down hard to reduce and concentrate it, and then spoon it generously over the squid.

PER SERVING: Energy 256kcal/1079kJ; Protein 24.6g; Carbohydrate 11.9g, of which sugars 0.7g; Fat 8.3g, of which saturates 1.4g; Cholesterol 338mg; Calcium 41mg; Fibre 0.3g; Sodium 263mg.

Serves 4

675g/1½lb white fish fillets, such as
    pike, carp or perch
40g/1½oz/¼ cup raisins
30ml/2 tbsp lemon juice
30ml/2 tbsp cold water
45ml/3 tbsp olive oil
2 onions, peeled and sliced
2 leeks, thinly sliced
2 garlic cloves, crushed
1 carrot, peeled and diced
115g/4oz green beans, cut into
    2.5cm/1in lengths
60ml/4 tbsp chopped fresh dill
salt and ground black pepper

VARIATION

This layered fish and vegetable bake can
also be made with skinned and boned
eel and is delicious sprinkled with
butter-fried breadcrumbs.

Piran Baked Fish
Pečena riba po piransko

The old seaport of Piran lies at the tip of the peninsula
on the Slovene coastline. This beautiful historic town
welcomes many visitors every year, who are treated to
the delightful taste of this unusual baked fish and
vegetable dish, served in many local restaurants.

1 Preheat the oven to 180°C/350°F/
Gas 4. Grease an ovenproof dish and
arrange the fish fillets in a single
layer along the bottom.

2 Put the raisins in a small bowl with
the lemon juice and the water. Leave
to soak for a few minutes while
cooking the vegetables.

3 Heat the olive oil in a frying pan
and gently cook the onions and leeks
for 5 minutes, until they begin to
soften. Stir in the garlic, carrot and
green beans and cook for an
additional 3–4 minutes.

4 Add the raisins and soaking liquid.
Gently heat until they are piping hot.
Season with salt and a few twists of
ground black pepper to taste.

5 Spoon the vegetable mixture over
the fish and then tightly cover with a
piece of foil. Bake for 20–25 minutes,
or until the fish and vegetables are
tender and cooked.

6 Sprinkle the top of the fish with the
chopped dill before serving this dish
with a generous helping of polenta
(see page 58) or some steamed
tender new potatoes.

PER SERVING: Energy 373kcal/1564kJ; Protein 33.5g; Carbohydrate 22.5g, of which sugars 19.3g; Fat 17.3g, of which saturates 2.9g; Cholesterol 113mg; Calcium 149mg; Fibre 5.3g; Sodium 97mg.

Marinated Fish

Ribe v šavorju

Shallow-frying little sea fish such as anchovies or picarel (a tiny member of the bream family), then marinating them is a popular way of serving fish in the Littoral area of Slovenia. This method can also be used for sprats and sardines, or fillets of fish such as red mullet and mackerel. Serve with crusty bread and a big green salad.

Serves 6

1kg/2¼lb anchovies or other small fish
plain (all-purpose) flour, for coating
olive oil, for frying
1 onion, sliced thinly
4 garlic cloves, crushed
30ml/2 tbsp fresh white breadcrumbs
4 ripe tomatoes, skinned and diced
1 bay leaf
1 fresh rosemary sprig
15ml/1 tbsp wine vinegar
salt and ground black pepper

COOK'S TIP

To skin the tomatoes, place them in a heatproof bowl and pour over boiling water to cover. Leave them for a minute, then drain and briefly rinse under cold water to cool. The skins should now slip off easily. Do not use tomato in the marinade mixture if you are preparing picarels or red mullet.

1 To prepare the anchovies, pinch the heads and pull them off; the guts should come out easily with them. Then pinch along the top edge of each fish and pull out the bony spine.

2 Rinse the fish and dry them on kitchen paper. Roll them in flour, lightly seasoned with salt and pepper, until they are evenly coated.

3 Pour a good layer of olive oil into a large, fairly deep frying pan. Heat the oil and fry the fish in batches, turning once, until they are lightly browned. Drain the fried fish on kitchen paper and set them aside as they are cooked.

4 Discard the used oil, wipe out the pan and heat 30ml/2 tbsp fresh olive oil in it. Gently fry the onion and garlic in the oil for about 10 minutes, or until the onion is softened.

5 Add the breadcrumbs, tomatoes, bay leaf and the fresh rosemary sprig. Season with salt and ground black pepper. Cook, stirring frequently, until the tomatoes are tender.

6 Stir in the wine vinegar and bring to the boil. Taste at this point, and add a little water if the mixture is too rich.

7 Place the fish in a suitable dish, packing them closely together. Spoon the tomato mixture over the fish (they should be completely covered).

8 Leave until cool, then cover the dish, place in the refrigerator and leave for 24 hours to allow the flavours to permeate the fish. Be sure to eat within 2 days.

PER SERVING: Energy 343kcal/1427kJ; Protein 26.7g; Carbohydrate 5.9g, of which sugars 2.2g; Fat 23.6g, of which saturates 4.9g; Cholesterol 0mg; Calcium 138mg; Fibre 0.8g; Sodium 186mg.

Serves 4–6

1.5kg/3lb whole pike
1 bay leaf
15ml/1 tbsp olive oil
50g/2oz/¼ cup butter
1 onion, chopped
1 garlic clove, chopped
115g/4oz/1½ cups wild mushrooms, thickly sliced
15ml/1 tbsp plain (all-purpose) flour
175ml/6fl oz/¾ cup sour cream
15ml/1 tbsp chopped fresh parsley
salt and ground black pepper

Baked Pike in Sour Cream
Pečena ščuka s kislo smetano

This freshwater fish has lean creamy-white flesh and needs to be kept moist during cooking. Here it is gently baked in a creamy sauce. Serve with sautéed potatoes.

VARIATION
Any large firm-fleshed white fish may be used here, such as perch or carp.

1 Preheat the oven to 190ºC/375ºF/ Gas 5. Clean, skin and fillet the pike, putting the bones and skin into a pan. Pour over just enough cold water to cover (use a little white wine instead of some of the water, if you wish) and add the bay leaf. Slowly bring to the boil, reduce the heat and gently simmer, uncovered, for 20 minutes.

2 Heat the oil and half the butter in a frying pan and cook the onion for 7–8 minutes, until soft. Add the garlic and mushrooms and cook for 2 more minutes. Strain the fish stock and reserve 300ml/½ pint/1¼ cups. Add the stock to the onion and mushroom mixture and simmer for 5 minutes.

3 Use the remaining butter to thickly grease an ovenproof dish. Arrange the fillets snugly in the dish and season with salt and pepper.

4 Blend the flour with the sour cream and pour into the onion and mushroom mixture. Bring to the boil, stirring, and carefully pour over the fish. Cover the dish with foil and bake for 30 minutes, until the fish is tender. Sprinkle with parsley.

PER SERVING: Energy 310kcal/1299kJ; Protein 40.2g; Carbohydrate 3.1g, of which sugars 1.2g; Fat 15.3g, of which saturates 5.7g; Cholesterol 178mg; Calcium 92mg; Fibre 0.3g; Sodium 158mg.

Fish Goulash

Ribji golaž

A remnant of Austro-Hungarian rule, goulash remains a
favourite and is often made with fish rather than meat.
It is flavoured with paprika and served with sour cream.

Serves 4

1.2kg/2½lb mixed fish
2 bay leaves
30ml/2 tbsp olive oil
1 large onion, chopped
2 celery sticks, chopped
1 green (bell) pepper, seeded and chopped
2 garlic cloves, chopped
75g/3oz lean smoked back bacon
    rashers (strips), rinded and diced
15ml/1 tbsp plain (all-purpose) flour
15ml/1 tbsp paprika, plus extra for sprinkling
5ml/1 tsp chopped fresh thyme
200g/7oz can chopped tomatoes
75g/3oz fine green beans, cut into
    bitesize lengths
30ml/2 tbsp chopped fresh parsley
salt and ground black pepper
sour cream, to serve

1 Skin and fillet the fish and cut the
flesh into large chunks. Put all the
fish bones into a large pan together
with the bay leaves. Barely cover with
cold water and bring to the boil.
Gently simmer for 30 minutes,
skimming the surface occasionally.
Strain the stock.

2 Heat the oil in a large pan, add the
onion and gently cook for 5 minutes.
Stir in the celery, green pepper,
garlic and bacon, and cook for a
further 3–4 minutes. Stir in the flour
and paprika and cook for 1 more
minute. Gradually add 600ml/1 pint/
2½ cups of the fish stock.

3 Add the thyme and chopped
tomatoes and then season with salt
and pepper. Cover and simmer for
5 minutes or until the vegetables are
almost tender

4 Add the green beans, fish chunks
and parsley and cook for about 10
minutes or until the fish and all the
vegetables are cooked. Ladle into
warmed deep plates or bowls and
serve with a generous spoonful of
sour cream and a sprinkle of paprika.

PER SERVING: Energy 382kcal/1603kJ; Protein 60.2g; Carbohydrate 9.4g, of which sugars 4.9g; Fat 11.7g, of which saturates 2.4g; Cholesterol 148mg; Calcium 60mg; Fibre 1.9g; Sodium 486mg.

Oven-roasted Carp
Pečeni krap

This freshwater fish has a firm flesh and is delicious when it is cooked on a base of sliced local new potatoes and caramelized white onions. The fish is covered with smoked streaky bacon before being baked in the oven, which helps to seal in the flavour and baste the fish as it cooks. The dish is delectable served with a helping of steamed green cabbage.

Serves 4

25g/1oz/2 tbsp butter, preferably unsalted
500g/1¼lb new potatoes
15ml/1 tbsp olive oil
1 large onion, thinly sliced
1 garlic clove, crushed
10ml/2 tsp cider vinegar
about 900g/2lb whole carp, cleaned
115g/4oz rindless smoked streaky (fatty) bacon rashers (strips)
salt and ground black pepper

COOK'S TIP

White fish and salty smoked bacon is always a good combination and is popular throughout central and Eastern Europe.

VARIATION

Any large, firm-fleshed white fish may be used in this recipe. Perch, tench, pike and cod will all work well, so you can use your local ingredients.

1 Preheat the oven to 180°C/350°F/Gas 4. Use half of the butter to thickly grease an ovenproof dish (the dish needs to be large enough to fit the fish fillets in along the bottom, side by side).

2 Bring a large pan of lightly salted water to the boil. Scrub the new potatoes and cut into 2cm/¾in thick slices. Add to the water, bring back to the boil and simmer for 10 minutes, until they are almost tender.

3 Remove from the pan with a slotted spoon and place in the bottom of the prepared dish. Spoon over 60ml/4 tbsp of the cooking liquid.

4 While the potatoes are cooking, heat the remaining butter and oil in a frying pan and gently cook the onions for 10 minutes over a medium heat until they are beginning to brown.

5 Add the garlic and cook for a further 2 minutes until just golden. Stir in the cider vinegar. Spoon the onions over the potatoes.

6 Place the carp fillets on top of the onions, then season with plenty of salt and pepper. Arrange the bacon rashers on top.

7 Cover the dish with foil and bake in the oven for 20 minutes, turning the dish halfway through cooking time to ensure even baking.

8 Remove the foil and bake for a further 15–20 minutes or until the bacon is browned and the fish is tender and flakes easily with a fork. Serve immediately with a generous helping of steamed green cabbage.

PER SERVING: Energy 438kcal/1836kJ; Protein 41.6g; Carbohydrate 20.1g, of which sugars 1.6g; Fat 21.8g, of which saturates 7.8g; Cholesterol 177mg; Calcium 64mg; Fibre 1.3g; Sodium 554mg.

DESSERTS AND BREADS

Krofi

Buckwheat Cheesecake

Bled Cream Slices

Poppy Potica

The Pohorje Omelette

Apple Batter Pudding

Pancakes with Pear Compote

Prekmurje Gibanica Pie

Walnut Syrup Cake

Bread with Olives

Rye Bread

Bosman Plaited Bread

Heavenly sweets and delicious breads

Slovenes have a particularly soft spot for sweet cakes, pastries, breads and desserts. After a hard day's walking or skiing in the mountains, what could be better than a warming dessert such as apple batter pudding, or baked pancakes rolled around a creamy filling with poached pears? On a hot day, it is tempting to try the Slovene version of ice cream, which often contains curd cheese as well as cream to give it that typically sharp/sweet taste. Ice creams of all flavours and other snacks such as doughnuts (krofi) are available to eat on the street, while strolling around picturesque towns and villages.

There are many elaborate traditional recipes for savoury and sweet loaves, made for special occasions such as birthdays, weddings or religious feast days. Rustic bread, too, made with unrefined flour, benefits from the addition of savoury or sweet fillings made of olives, figs, herbs and spices. The famous Slovene recipe, potica, a rolled bread stuffed with nuts, curd cheese and spices and bound with sugar, is essential at Christmas and Easter celebrations.

Makes 12
225g/8oz/2 cups strong white bread flour
large pinch of salt
7g/¼oz sachet easy-blend (rapid-rise)
    dried yeast
finely grated rind of ½ lemon
1 egg, lightly beaten
60–75ml/4–5 tbsp milk
about 45ml/3 tbsp apricot or plum jam
vegetable oil, for deep frying
50g/2oz/¼ cup caster (superfine) sugar
5ml/1 tsp ground cinnamon

COOK'S TIPS
• The krofi are best served still warm,
but let them cool for at least 10 minutes
first: the jam will be boiling hot.
• When deep-frying the krofi, turn them
several times in the hot oil to ensure they
brown evenly all over.

Krofi
Krofi

These deep-fried doughnut-like rolls are made for
special days. Usually flavoured with lemon, the dough is
unsweetened, so they may be a sweet or savoury treat.
In this version they're filled with jam, but you could leave
this out and roll in finely grated Parmesan after cooking.

1 Sift the flour and salt into a bowl.
Stir in the yeast and lemon rind. Make
a well in the middle and add the egg
and milk. Mix to make a soft dough.

2 Turn the dough out on to a lightly
floured surface, kneading for 3–4
minutes until smooth and elastic.
Divide into 12 equal-sized pieces.

3 Shape each piece into a round about
7.5cm/3in across, then put less than
5ml/1 tsp jam in the middle. Dampen
the edges of the dough with water,
then pull together and pinch firmly to
seal in the jam and make a ball.

4 Place the balls on a greased baking
sheet. Leave to rise in a warm place
for 30 minutes, or until doubled in size.

5 Half-fill a large pan with oil. Heat to
180°C/350°F. Fry the krofi for 6–8
minutes, until deep-golden brown.
Remove and drain on kitchen paper.

6 While the krofi are still hot, mix the
sugar and cinnamon on a plate and
roll the krofi, coating evenly all over.

PER SERVING: Energy 173kcal/724kJ; Protein 2.5g; Carbohydrate 21.8g, of which sugars 7.5g; Fat 9g, of which saturates 1.1g; Cholesterol 16mg; Calcium 37mg; Fibre 0.6g; Sodium 10mg.

Serves 8

For the pastry

100g/3¾oz/scant 1 cup buckwheat flour

100g/3¾oz/scant 1 cup plain
(all-purpose) flour

115g/4oz/½ cup butter, diced

1 egg yolk

15–30ml/1–2 tbsp chilled water

For the filling

500g/1¼lb curd (farmer's) cheese

115g/4oz/⅔ cup caster (superfine) sugar

3 eggs, lightly beaten

150ml/¼ pint/⅔ cup sour cream

30ml/2 tbsp plain (all-purpose) flour

VARIATION

To make a savoury cheesecake, leave out
the sugar and season the filling with a
pinch of salt and black pepper.

Buckwheat Cheesecake
Ajdova zlevanka

This light cheesecake, made with a butter-rich pastry
crust, is usually served with coffee or enjoyed as an
afternoon treat with a small glass of wine. It is also
perfect as a dessert, finished with a simple dusting of
icing sugar or topped with fresh glazed fruit.

1 Place a baking sheet in the oven
and preheat to 190°C/375°F/Gas 5.
Sift the flours into a bowl and rub in
the butter until the mixture takes
on the texture of fine breadcrumbs.

2 Stir the egg yolk into the flour and
add just enough of the water to bind
the mixture together to make a
dough. Wrap the pastry in clear film
(plastic wrap). Chill for 20 minutes.

3 Roll out the pastry on a floured
surface and line a 20cm/8in fluted
loose-based flan tin (quiche pan). Add
baking parchment, add dried beans
or rice and blind bake for 10 minutes.

4 For the filling, beat the curd cheese
and sugar together, then beat in the
eggs, a little at a time. Stir in two-
thirds of the sour cream. Sift the flour
over the surface and gently fold it in.

5 Spoon the cheese mixture on to the
pastry and spread evenly. Spread the
remaining sour cream evenly over
the top. Bake the cheesecake for
about 40 minutes, until the filling is
lightly set (it will firm more as it cools)
and the top is pale golden-brown.

6 Leave to cool in the pan and serve
while still slightly warm, or cold with
extra sour cream, if you like.

PER SERVING: Energy 403kcal/1685kJ; Protein 14.9g; Carbohydrate 37.1g, of which sugars 18.1g; Fat 23.7g, of which saturates 14.2g; Cholesterol 156mg; Calcium 135mg; Fibre 1.9g; Sodium 418mg.

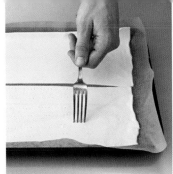

Bled Cream Slices
Blejska kremna rezina

A baker's son once brought recipes back from his travels in Germany and Austria. One was a delicious confection with layers of buttery pastry sandwiching vanilla custard and cream. Pastry chefs at the Park Hotel in Bled took this idea and created the 'best cream cake in the world', serving eight million slices in 50 years. Now you can make it at home.

Makes 10 slices
450g/1lb puff pastry
300ml/½ pint/1¼ cups milk
pared strip of lemon rind
3 egg yolks
50g/2oz/4 tbsp caster (superfine) sugar
35g/1¼oz/generous ¼ cup plain
   (all-purpose) flour
1 egg white
450ml/¾ pint/scant 2 cups double
   (heavy) cream
15ml/1 tbsp rum
5ml/1 tsp vanilla extract
45ml/3 tbsp icing (confectioners') sugar

1 Remove the pastry from the refrigerator and leave it, still wrapped, at room temperature for 20 minutes. Roll out on a lightly floured surface to an oblong 30 x 37.5cm/12 x 15in. Trim the pastry edges neatly, then prick all over with a fork. Cut into two rectangles, each one 15 x 37.5cm/6 x 15in.

2 Place the pastry on a large baking sheet lined with baking paper and mark one rectangle into ten 7.5cm/3in squares, carefully cutting no more than halfway through the pastry. Chill in the refrigerator for at least 30 minutes.

3 While the pastry is chilling, start making the pastry cream. Put the milk and lemon rind in a small heavy pan and slowly bring to the boil. Whisk the egg yolks and 15g/½oz/1 tbsp caster sugar in a bowl until thick and pale. Sift the flour and stir in.

4 Remove the lemon rind from the milk and whisk the hot milk into the egg and flour mixture. Pour back into the pan. Thicken the custard by stirring over a low heat. Pour into a bowl, then cover. Leave until just cool, but not firmly set.

5 Whisk the egg white until stiff and whisk in the remaining caster sugar. Whip 150ml/¼ pint/⅔ cup of the cream until thick. Stir the rum into the custard. Gently fold the egg white mixture into the custard, followed by the whipped cream. Cover with cling film (plastic wrap) and chill for 30 minutes.

6 Preheat the oven to 220°C/425°F/Gas 7. Dampen the baking sheets around the pastry with cold water. Bake for 25 minutes, until well-risen and golden. Cool.

7 Pour 300ml/½ pint/1¼ cups cream into a chilled bowl. Add the vanilla extract and sift over 15ml/1 tbsp icing (confectioners') sugar. Whip the remaining cream.

8 Place the unmarked pastry sheet on a board and spread with the pastry cream, then the whipped cream. Put the marked pastry sheet on top. Dust with icing sugar.

PER SERVING: Energy 436kcal/1812kJ; Protein 5.8g; Carbohydrate 26.8g, of which sugars 8.1g; Fat 37.4g, of which saturates 14.3g; Cholesterol 121mg; Calcium 99mg; Fibre 0.1g; Sodium 182mg.

Poppy Potica
Makova potica

Potica (or povitica) is made to share at celebratory events and holidays such as weddings, Christmas, New Year and Easter. It is often made with walnuts (see variation below), but there are many varieties, including this poppy seed one. A slice is often given to children on their first day of the new school year in the hope of making them smarter.

Makes 1 large loaf
75g/3oz/scant ½ cup caster (superfine) sugar
25g/1oz fresh yeast
250ml/8fl oz/1 cup lukewarm milk
300g/11oz/2¾ cups plain (all-purpose) flour, warmed
5ml/1 tsp salt
2 egg yolks
5ml/1 tsp vanilla extract
30ml/2 tbsp vegetable oil
5ml/1 tsp rum
grated rind of 1 lemon
65g/2½oz/5 tbsp butter, melted
1 egg yolk, lightly beaten for glazing
icing (confectioners') sugar, for sprinkling (optional)

Poppy filling
200g/7oz/¾ cup poppy seeds, ground
150g/5oz/¾ cup sugar
5ml/1 tsp vanilla extract
45ml/3 tbsp rum
grated rind of 1 lemon
5ml/1 tsp ground cinnamon
40g/1½oz/3 tbsp butter, melted
75g/2½oz/½ cup raisins (optional)

1 Mix 10ml/2 tsp of the sugar with the yeast, then stir in 60ml/4 tbsp of the milk. Set aside in a warm place for about 15 minutes, until frothy.

2 Place the flour in a bowl with the salt. Make a well in the middle and pour in the yeast liquid, then stir in just a little of the flour.

3 Beat the egg yolks with the remaining sugar, the vanilla extract, oil, rum and lemon rind, then stir in the remaining milk and melted butter. Pour this mixture into the bowl and stir it into the yeast liquid, then gradually stir in the flour, mixing it into a dough. Work the dough by hand in the bowl until it comes away from the sides of the bowl easily.

4 Turn the dough out on to a floured surface and knead thoroughly until smooth and elastic. Return the dough to the bowl, cover with a cloth and leave in a warm place until it has doubled in size – about 1½ hours.

5 Meanwhile, grease a large oblong baking tin (pan), measuring about 40 x 10cm/16 x 4in, and prepare the filling. Mix the ground poppy seeds with the sugar, vanilla extract, rum, lemon rind or juice and cinnamon.

6 Knock back the risen dough by kneading it briefly, then roll it out on a floured surface into a 1cm/⅜in thick rectangle. The longer side of the rectangle should measure slightly less than 40cm/16in.

7 Spread the poppy seed mixture over the dough, then drizzle the melted butter evenly over the filling. Sprinkle raisins over the filling, if you wish. Roll up the dough firmly and place it in the greased pan. Pierce the potica with a trussing needle or fine metal skewer in several places, then cover it with a cloth and leave it to rise in a warm place for about 1½ hours.

PER LOAF : Energy 4463kcal/18678kJ; Protein 82.5g; Carbohydrate 487.8g, of which sugars 252.9g; Fat 244.8g, of which saturates 82.1g; Cholesterol 660mg; Calcium 2269mg; Fibre 25.1g; Sodium 1011mg.

COOK'S TIPS

• One and a half x 7g/¼oz sachets of easy-blend (rapid-rise) yeast may be used instead of the fresh yeast. Mix with the flour, salt and sugar in the bowl.

• Originally, ceramic moulds with a cone-shaped centre were used for baking potica. A steel kugelhopf mould is similar in shape and may be used instead (and can also be used for jellies or mousses). If you haven't got a suitable-sized tin, bake the potica, seam side down on a well-greased baking sheet.

8 Preheat the oven to 180°C/350°F/Gas 4. Brush the risen potica with egg yolk and bake for 40–50 minutes, until golden brown. Leave the potica to cool in the tin for 15 minutes, then turn it out of the tin on to a board and cover it with a cloth. Leave to cool. Sprinkle with a little sugar, if you like, before serving.

VARIATIONS

• For a walnut filling, mix 250g/9oz/1½ cups walnuts, finely ground, with 5ml/2fl oz/ ¼ cup rum or whisky, 50g/2oz/¼ cup caster (superfine) sugar and 45ml/3 tbsp double (heavy) cream.

• For a tarragon filling, cream 175g/6oz softened butter with 45ml/3 tsp caster sugar until light. Beat in 2 egg yolks, one at a time, then stir in 2 bunches of trimmed and chopped fresh tarragon. Whisk the egg whites until they are fairly stiff and carefully fold into the mixture.

Serves 1–2

25g/1oz/2 tbsp butter, preferably
  unsalted, for greasing
25g/1oz/¼ cup plain (all-purpose) flour
75g/3oz/¾ cup fresh or
  frozen cranberries
3 egg whites
50g/2oz/¼ cup sugar, plus 30ml/2 tbsp
2 egg yolks
15ml/1 tbsp vanilla sugar
grated rind of 1 lemon
120ml/4fl oz/½ cup double (heavy) cream
25g/1oz/¼ cup icing
  (confectioners') sugar
30ml/2 tbsp cranberry liqueur,
  grenadine or other fruit liqueur

The Pohorje Omelette
Pohorska omleta

Cranberries fill this classic baked omelette. Variations
include fresh cherries and dark bitter chocolate.

1 Preheat the oven to 200°C/400°F/
Gas 6. Butter a round ovenproof tin
(pan) 25cm/10in in diameter and
sprinkle with flour. Shake the flour
around the tin and tip out any excess.

2 Put the cranberries, 30ml/2 tbsp of
sugar and 15ml/1 tbsp water in a pan
and heat gently until the sugar has
melted. Cook for about 10 minutes or
until the cranberries are tender.

3 Using an electric beater, whisk the
egg whites until stiff. Slowly add the
sugar, whisking continuously until
the mixture is stiff and glossy.

4 Lightly beat the egg yolks with the
vanilla sugar in a small bowl, then fold
into the whites with the lemon rind
and flour. Transfer to the prepared
pan and bake for 10 minutes, until set.

5 Meanwhile, whip the cream with
most of the icing sugar until it stands
in soft peaks.

6 Top the omelette with berries as
soon as it comes out of the oven and
fold in half. Slide the omelette on to a
plate and sift icing sugar over it.
Decorate with whipped cream, pour
the liqueur over the top and serve.

PER SERVING: Energy 712kcal/2974kJ; Protein 9.8g; Carbohydrate 66.6g, of which sugars 57.1g; Fat 48.1g, of which saturates 26.4g; Cholesterol 308mg; Calcium 102mg; Fibre 1g; Sodium 222mg.

Serves 4

30ml/2 tbsp sunflower oil

450g/1lb eating apples, peeled, cored
and thickly sliced

115g/4oz/1 cup plain (all-purpose) flour

pinch of salt

5ml/1 tsp ground cinnamon

50g/2oz/¼ cup caster (superfine) sugar

1 egg

300ml/½ pint/1¼ cups milk

15ml/1 tbsp icing (confectioners') sugar

Apple Batter Pudding

Jabolčna pita

Quick and simple to make, this pudding is also good made with pears, plums or cherries.
Serve with cream whipped with a dash of fruit liqueur, or scoops of vanilla ice cream.

1 Preheat the oven to 220°C/425°F/
Gas 7. Pour the oil in a roasting pan,
about 25 x 30cm/10 x 12in, and swirl
around the base and up the sides to
coat evenly. Add the apple slices,
spreading them out evenly. Put the
pan in the oven for 10 minutes.

2 Meanwhile, make the batter. Sift
the flour, salt and cinnamon into a
bowl. Stir in the sugar, then make
a well in the middle. Add the egg and
gradually whisk in the milk to make
a smooth batter.

3 Remove the pan from the oven and
pour the batter over the apples.
Return to the oven and bake for
25–30 minutes, until well-risen and
dark golden-brown. Dust with icing
(confectioners') sugar. Serve at once.

VARIATION

For a savoury batter pudding, lightly
grease four shallow ovenproof dishes,
each 15cm/6in. Divide 450g/1lb cherry
tomatoes and 50g/2oz grated Parmesan
between them. Make the batter as before,
leaving out the sugar and stirring in
45ml/3 tbsp chopped fresh chives, salt
and pepper. Pour over the batter and bake
at 190°C/375°F/Gas 5 for 35 minutes.

PER SERVING: Energy 304kcal/1286kJ; Protein 7.2g; Carbohydrate 53.1g, of which sugars 31.2g; Fat 8.7g, of which saturates 1.9g; Cholesterol 52mg; Calcium 151mg; Fibre 2.7g; Sodium 63mg.

Pancakes with Pear Compote
Palačinke s hruševim kompotom

Pancakes are much loved in Slovenia and are made into many sweet and savoury dishes. Here, lacy, lemon-scented pancakes are rolled around a plum jam and almond filling, drizzled in cream and then baked. They are served with thickly sliced pears that have been poached in a syrupy red wine sauce.

Serves 4

For the pancakes
115g/4oz/1 cup plain (all-purpose) flour
pinch of salt
finely grated rind of 1 lemon
1 egg
300ml/½ pint/1¼ cups milk
oil, for frying
30ml/2 tbsp icing (confectioners') sugar, to serve
toasted flaked almonds, to serve

For the filling
45ml/3 tbsp good-quality plum jam
75g/3oz/¾ cup flaked (sliced) almonds
150ml/¼ pint/⅔ cup single (light) cream

For the poached pear compote
4 firm, ripe pears, peeled, halved, cored and thickly sliced
30ml/2 tbsp lemon juice
45ml/3 tbsp redcurrant jelly
75ml/2½fl oz/⅓ cup fruity red wine

VARIATION

Try poaching other fresh fruit, when it is in season. Halved apricots or peaches are especially delicious when they are poached in a white or rosé wine.

1 To make the pancakes, sift the flour and salt into a bowl and stir in the lemon rind. Make a well in the centre, add the egg, then whisk in the milk to make up a smooth batter. Cover and leave to stand, if possible, for about 15 minutes.

2 Brush an 18cm/7in non-stick frying pan with a little oil, then heat. Add about one-eighth of the batter and tilt the pan so that the batter coats the bottom thinly and evenly. Cook for about 1 minute, or until the pancake has set and the underside is lightly browned. Turn or toss the pancake and cook the second side for 45 seconds until golden.

3 Transfer the pancake to a plate. Repeat with the rest of the batter, stacking the cooked pancakes as you finish making them, interleaving them with sheets of baking parchment.

4 Preheat the oven to 180°C/350°F/Gas 4. Spread each pancake with just a little of the jam, then sprinkle with almonds. Roll them up and arrange them seam side down in a single layer in a greased ovenproof dish.

5 Carefully pour the cream over the pancakes. Cover the dish with foil and bake in the oven for about 20 minutes.

6 While the pancakes are baking, prepare the pears. Toss the pear slices in the lemon juice. Gently heat the redcurrant jelly and wine in a wide shallow pan until the jelly has melted. Add the pear slices and gently cook for 6–7 minutes or until they are tender.

7 Remove the pears with a slotted spoon and transfer to a bowl. Turn up the heat and let the wine mixture bubble for about 5 minutes until it is reduced by half. Pour over the pears. Serve the hot pancakes, sprinkled with the toasted flaked almonds and icing sugar, with the poached pears.

PER SERVING: Energy 575kcal/2410kJ; Protein 12.3g; Carbohydrate 67.4g, of which sugars 45g; Fat 29.1g, of which saturates 7.7g; Cholesterol 73mg; Calcium 242mg; Fibre 5.6g; Sodium 91mg.

Prekmurje Gibanica Pie
Prekmurska gibanica

This celebrated multi-layered and flavoured Slovene dessert is a traditional festive dish in Prekmurje, in the extreme north-eastern part of the country. Written recipes dating as far back as 1828 have been discovered, although the dish was probably created long before then.

Serves 12–14

For the flan pastry base
175g/6oz/1½ cups plain
  (all-purpose) flour
pinch of salt
large pinch of caster (superfine) sugar
75g/3oz/6 tbsp chilled butter, diced
1 egg yolk
15ml/1 tbsp chilled water

For the filo pastry
450g/1lb/4 cups strong white
  bread flour
5ml/1 tsp salt
2 eggs, lightly beaten
20ml/4 tsp sunflower oil
about 300ml/½ pint/1¼ cups slightly
  warm water
50g/2oz/¼ cup butter, melted, for
  brushing, plus extra for greasing

For the apple filling
450g/1lb apples, quartered, peeled, cored
and thinly sliced
2.5ml/½ tsp ground cinnamon
25g/1oz/2 tbsp caster sugar
50g/2oz/1 cup fresh white breadcrumbs

For the sour cream mixture
2 eggs, separated
300ml/½ pint/1¼ cups sour cream

1 To make the flan pastry, sift the flour, salt and sugar into a bowl. Rub or cut in the butter until the mixture resembles fine breadcrumbs. Mix together the egg yolk and water, sprinkle over the dry ingredients and stir in with a fork. Gather the mixture together with your hands, adding more water if needed. Lightly knead for a minute, or until smooth. Shape into a ball, then flatten into a round. Wrap in clear film (plastic wrap) and chill for 30 minutes.

2 For the filo pastry, sift the flour and salt into a mixing bowl. Make a well and stir the eggs and oil into the water, add to the flour and mix to form a sticky dough. 'Beat' the dough by lifting and slapping it down on to a lightly floured surface. Continue until it no longer sticks to your fingers, then knead for 5 minutes until smooth and elastic. Shape into a ball, place on a dish towel and cover with an upturned bowl. Leave to rest at room temperature for 30 minutes.

3 For the apple filling, put the apple slices in a heavy pan with the cinnamon. Half-cover the pan with a lid and cook for 10–15 minutes, stirring occasionally until the apples are tender. Stir in the sugar and breadcrumbs. Leave to cool.

4 For the curd filling, put the raisins in a bowl with boiling water. Leave to cool, then drain the raisins. Mix the curd cheese, sugar and vanilla together in a bowl, then stir in the raisins. For the walnut filling, put everything into a bowl and stir together. For the poppy filling, put the ground seeds, sugar and lemon rind in a bowl. Scald the milk and pour over, stirring well.

5 To make the sour cream mixture, mix the egg yolks and sour cream. Whisk the whites until stiff; gently fold in. Spoon 60ml/4 tbsp of the mixture into a bowl. Divide the rest between the curd, walnut and poppy fillings. Gently fold in.

6 Put a baking sheet in an oven preheated to 180°C/350°F/Gas 4. Butter a round pan 25cm/10in wide and 9cm/3½in high. Roll out the flan pastry to a round larger than the pan. Lift into the pan, pushing the pastry up the sides.

PER SERVING: Energy 326kcal/1369kJ; Protein 7.4g; Carbohydrate 43g, of which sugars 6.3g; Fat 15.1g, of which saturates 8.3g; Cholesterol 102mg; Calcium 100mg; Fibre 2g; Sodium 126mg.

For the curd filling
75g/3oz/scant ½ cup raisins
50g/2oz/¼ cup caster sugar
350g/12oz/½ cups curd (farmer's) cheese
5ml/1 tsp vanilla extract

For the walnut filling
200g/7oz ground walnuts
50g/2oz/¼ cup caster sugar
45ml/3 tbsp rum

For the poppy filling
200g/7oz poppy seeds, finely ground
50g/2oz/¼ cup caster sugar
finely grated rind of ½ lemon
60ml/4 tbsp milk

7 Spoon half the poppy mixture into the pan and spread out into an even layer. Divide the filo pastry into ten equal pieces. Keep nine pieces covered with a damp dish towel and thinly roll out one piece to a round just slightly larger than the pan (see page 18), then trim the thick edges with kitchen scissors. Carefully place on top of the poppy seed filling; again the edges should come just a little way up the sides of the pan. Lightly brush the filo with melted butter.

8 Top the filo layer with half of the curd filling, then top with filo and brush with butter, as before. Follow with half of the walnut filling, filo and butter and then the apple filling, filo and butter. Repeat all the layers again with the remaining fillings, pastry and butter.

9 Add two more layers of filo pastry, buttering between the layers, then spoon the reserved sour cream mixture over the top. Pierce the gibanica in several places with a very fine skewer, right through the layers to the bottom.

10 Bake in the oven for 1 hour, until the top is golden brown, loosely covering the top with foil if it over-browns. Serve cold or slightly warm, cut into wedges.

Makes 8–12 slices
175g/6oz/1½ cups walnut pieces
150g/5oz/10 tbsp butter, softened
150g/5oz/⅔ cup soft light brown sugar
60ml/4 tbsp set honey
3 eggs, lightly beaten
5ml/1 tsp vanilla extract
50g/2oz/½ cup plain (all-purpose) flour
50g/2oz/½ cup wholemeal
  (whole-wheat) flour
5ml/1 tsp baking powder
5ml/1 tsp ground cinnamon
65g/2½oz/generous ½ cup polenta
75ml/5ml milk
90g/3½oz/½ cup golden caster
  (superfine) sugar
60ml/4 tbsp set honey
120ml/4fl oz/½ cup water
pinch of salt

Walnut Syrup Cake
Orehove rezine

This moist cake, drizzled with sticky syrup, is typical of a
Slovene sweet treat. Serve in thin slices with coffee.

1 Preheat the oven to 180°C/350°F/
Gas 4. Grease and line a 20cm/8in
round cake tin (pan). Place the walnut
pieces on a baking tray and roast for
8–10 minutes, until slightly darker and
aromatic. Cool, then roughly chop.

2 Put the butter, sugar and honey in
a bowl and beat until light and fluffy.
Gradually add the eggs, beating well.
Beat in the vanilla extract.

3 Sift the flours, baking powder, salt
and cinnamon over the mixture,
adding any bran left in the sieve
(strainer). Fold in and when half-mixed
add the nuts, polenta and milk. Fold in.

4 Spoon the mixture into the prepared
tin (pan) and level the surface. Bake
for 45–50 minutes, or until well-risen,
firm and lightly browned.

5 Make the syrup. Put the sugar, honey
and water in a pan. Gently heat and
stir until the sugar has dissolved.
Simmer for 5 minutes. Turn off the heat.

6 When the cake is ready, drizzle the
warm syrup evenly over the top.

PER CAKE: Energy 2519kcal/10686kJ; Protein 78.7g; Carbohydrate 508.3g, of which sugars 9.4g; Fat 33.1g, of which saturates 4.8g; Cholesterol 0mg; Calcium 1016mg; Fibre 24.3g; Sodium 6538mg.

Makes 1 loaf
15g/½oz fresh yeast
5ml/1 tsp sugar
675g/1½lb/6 cups strong white
   bread flour
10ml/2 tsp salt
475ml/16fl oz/2 cups warm water
15ml/1 tbsp olive oil, lard or white
   cooking fat
115g/4oz/1 cup pitted black olives,
   or dried figs, chopped

Bread with Olives
Kruh z oljkami

Once rare ingredients, such as olives or figs from Mediterranean Slovenia, are used to flavour this white bread, formerly a luxury that was baked only for special occasions.

1 Mix the yeast with the sugar, add 45ml/3 tbsp water and stir. Leave in a warm place for 15 minutes until frothy.

2 Put three-quarters of the flour in a big bowl. Make a well and add the salt, pour in the warm water and oil. Add the olives or figs and stir until the flour begins to mix with the liquid.

3 Pour in the yeasty liquid, mix to a sticky dough. Sprinkle some flour on to a work surface and knead the dough for 15 minutes; add the remaining flour.

4 Place the dough in a clean bowl, cover with a cloth and leave in a warm place for 1 hour, until doubled in size.

5 Turn the dough on to a floured surface. Knead again to knock out the air. Mould into a large oval, place on a greased baking sheet and cover with a cloth. Leave to rise for 20 to 30 minutes.

6 Preheat the oven to 150°C/300°F/Gas 3. Put the bread in; turn up to 200°C/400°F/ Gas 6. Bake for 45–60 minutes until brown. Turn the oven off and leave the bread in for 10 more minutes.

PER SERVING: Energy 362kcal/1514kJ; Protein 5g; Carbohydrate 39.2g, of which sugars 29.4g; Fat 21.6g, of which saturates 7.9g; Cholesterol 61mg; Calcium 47mg; Fibre 1.1g; Sodium 112mg.

Rye Bread
Rženi kruh

Rye is one of the most important crops throughout Eastern and Central Europe and this dark, dense-textured rye bread is typical of those made in Slovenia. Originally, it would have been made with a sourdough starter – a flour and water paste, left to ferment by airborne yeast.

Makes 2 medium loaves

250g/9oz/generous 2 cups rye flour, plus extra for dusting
250g/9oz/generous 2 cups plain (all-purpose) flour
about 300ml/½ pint/1¼ cups warm water
20g/¾oz fresh yeast
15ml/1 tbsp caster (superfine) sugar (optional)
10ml/2 tsp salt
75g/3oz lard or white cooking fat

VARIATION

To substitute easy-blend dried yeast in this recipe, stir 2.5ml/½ tsp easy-blend dried yeast into the flour when making the starter and 7.5ml/1½ tsp when making the main dough.

COOK'S TIPS

• The flavour of this bread develops and matures after baking and the loaves will keep for several days.
• Use dark rye flour to make the dough if you like a loaf with a strong distinctive flavour, light rye flour for a paler colour and milder taste.

1 To make the starter dough, combine the rye flour with the plain flour, put 150g/5oz of the flour into a bowl and make a hollow. Measure 150ml/¼ pint/⅔ cup of water into a jug (pitcher). Crumble in half of the yeast and stir until dissolved. Pour into the flour and mix to make a thick batter. Cover with a damp dish towel and leave at room temperature for 6–8 hours.

2 The following day, put the remaining flour in a large bowl. Stir in the sugar (if using) and salt, then rub in the lard or white fat with your fingertips.

3 Make a hollow in the middle of the flour and add the starter and most of the remaining water, along with the remaining yeast. Mix together to make a soft dough, adding the rest of the water if necessary.

4 Turn out the dough on a lightly floured surface and knead it hard for about 10 minutes, until it is smooth and elastic.

5 Put the dough in a clean bowl, cover with clear film (plastic wrap) and leave in a warm place to rise for an hour, or until it has doubled in size.

6 Turn out the dough again, re-knead, then divide into two equal pieces. Shape each into a long oval and transfer to two greased baking sheets. Cover with oiled cling film and leave to rise as before, for about an hour.

7 Meanwhile, preheat the oven to 220°C/425°F/Gas 7. Uncover the loaves, lightly dust the tops with rye flour and make diagonal parallel slashes on them about 5mm/¼in deep at 1cm/½in intervals.

8 Bake in the preheated oven for 25–35 minutes until the loaves are hollow-sounding when tapped underneath. Leave to cool on a wire rack, carefully covering the loaves with a clean towel to keep the crust soft.

PER LOAF: Energy 1046kcal/4429kJ; Protein 20.6g; Carbohydrate 197.6g, of which sugars 7.9g; Fat 24.8g, of which saturates 8.9g; Cholesterol 19mg; Calcium 85mg; Fibre 29.3g; Sodium 1969mg.

Bosman Plaited Bread

Bosman

This festive wedding bread is always made from the finest white flour. It is a complicated multi-braided loaf, but if you prefer, the dough may be divided into just three pieces and made into a simple plait. The loaf should be elaborately decorated with shapes that are fashioned from spare bread dough or with paper flowers, added after baking.

Makes 1 large loaf

800g/1¾lb/7 cups strong white bread flour
5ml/1 tsp salt
25ml/1½ tbsp easy-blend dried yeast
300ml/½ pint/1¼ cups warm water
45ml/3 tbsp clear honey
3 eggs, lightly beaten
75g/3oz/6 tbsp softened butter
1 egg yolk
15ml/1 tbsp cold water

1 Sift the flour and salt into a mixing bowl and stir in the yeast. Make a well in the middle and add the water, honey, eggs and butter. Mix everything together to make a soft dough.

2 Turn out the dough on a lightly floured surface and knead for 10 minutes, until smooth and elastic. Place the dough in a clean bowl and cover with cling film (plastic wrap). Leave to rise until doubled in size, about 2 hours.

3 Knock the dough back, then rest it for about 10 minutes. Divide the dough into ten equal pieces. Roll nine of the pieces into long sausage shapes that are about 30cm/12in long.

4 Plait (braid) four strands together and place on a greased baking sheet. Plait three more strands and place in the middle of the four-strand plait.

5 Roll the remaining two strands of dough just a little longer and then twist them together. Place this on top of the three-strand plait, tucking the ends under, so that everything is held together.

6 Use the remaining piece of dough to create decorations in the shapes of birds, flowers, butterflies, small braids and small balls.

VARIATION

For a shiny golden glaze, infuse (steep) a few strands of saffron in 15ml/1 tbsp hot milk. Strain when cool and mix with the egg yolk instead of the water.

7 Cover the bread with oiled cling film and leave it to rise for an hour or until doubled in size. Preheat the oven to 180°C/350°F/Gas 4. Mix the egg yolk and cold water together and carefully brush over the bread to glaze.

8 Bake for 45 minutes, until it is richly golden brown and hollow sounding when tapped underneath. Cool on a wire rack.

PER SERVING: Energy 3692kcal/15597kJ; Protein 97.4g; Carbohydrate 656g, of which sugars 46.4g; Fat 93.8g, of which saturates 48.3g; Cholesterol 945mg; Calcium 1243mg; Fibre 24.8g; Sodium 2775mg.

Useful Addresses

AUSTRALIA

Food shops and markets

Bosnus Convenience Store
5/107 Turpin Road, Labrador
4215, Gold Coast
www.bosnusconvenience.com

Polka Deli
22 Post Office Place, Glenroy,
VIC 3046
Tel: 03 9304 4700
www.polka.net.au/about.html

Polka Deli
Shop R04, Parkmore Shopping
Centre, Cheltenham Road,
Keysborough VIC 3173
Tel: 03 9798 8422
www.polka.net.au/about.html

Restaurants

Borsch i Vodka
38 David Street, Turner
ACT 2602
Tel: 61 2 6248 8563

Prague Czech Beer Restaurant
42 Kellett Street, Potts Point
NSW 2011
Tel: 61 2 9368 0898

V & V
136 Koornang Road,
Carnegie VIC 3163
Tel : 61 3 9568 1621
www.russianrestaurant.com.au

CANADA

Food shops and markets

Quality European Deli
1390 Walker Road, Windsor,
Ontario
Tel: 519-252-8243

Viking Deli & Smokehouse
133 Laird Drive, Toronto,
Ontario
Tel: 416-425-7200

Restaurants

Paprika
450 Bathurst St, Toronto,
Ontario,North York
Tel: 416-789-3478

Starskys
2040 Dundas St East,
Mississauga, Ontario
Tel: 905-279-8889
www.starskycanada.com

Tuske
586 Bloor St West, Toronto,
Ontario
Tel: 416-588-8014
www.tuskedeli.com/default.htm

Warmia
323 Roncesvalles Avenue,
Toronto, Ontario
Tel: 905-270-7182

UNITED KINGDOM

Food shops and markets

Polonium Deli
300 London Road, Sheffield S2 4NA
Tel: 01142 508989

Wally's Delicatessen
42–44 Royal Arcade,
Cardiff CF10 2AE
Tel: 02920 229265
www.wallysdeli.co.uk

Babushka (Derbyshire)
71 West Bars, Chesterfield,
Derbyshire S40 1BA
Tel: 01246 555336
www.babushkauk.com

Babushka (Mansfield)
12 Bridge Street,
Mansfield NG18 1AN.
Tel: 01623 628896
www.babushkauk.com

Babushka (Newark)
24 Portland Street,
Newark NG24 4XG
Tel: 01636 646914
www.babushkauk.com

P & K Deli
145 Bond Street, Blackpool,
Lancashire FY4 1HG
tel: 01253 341001
www.pkdeli.co.uk

Prima Delicatessen
192 North End Road, West
Kensington, London, W14 9NX
020 7385 2070

Restaurants

Wodka
12 St Albans Grove, London W8
Tel: 020 7937 6513

Zorya
48 Chalk Farm Road, Camden
Town, London NW1 8AJ
Tel: 020 7485 8484

Divo
12 Waterloo Place, St. James's,
London SW1Y 4AU
Tel: 020 7484 1355

The Sava Restaurant
358A Fulham Road, Black Bull,
Chelsea, London SW10 9UU
Tel: 020 7376 7370

UNITED STATES

Food shops and markets

Beograd Meat Market
2933-39 West Irving Park Road,
Northwest Side, Chicago
Tel: 773-478-7575

Delikateski
1984 Monument Boulevard,
Concord, California
Tel: 925-825-7417

Duke's Eatery and Deli
6312 S Harlem Ave,
Summit, Ilinois
Tel: 708-594-5622

Kiko's Market and Restaurant
5077 North Lincoln Avenue,
Lincoln Square/Ravenswood,
Chicago
Tel: 773-271-7006

Sunnyside Meat Market
3-10 43rd Street, Queens,
New York NY 11104
Tel: 718-786-2626

M & I International Food
49 Brighton Beach Avenue,
Brooklyn, New York NY 11235
Tel: 718-615-1011

Romanoff Supermarket
63-64 108th Street, Queens,
New York NY 11375
Tel: 718-897-3600

European Turkish Market
1138 Chula Vista Avenue,
Burlingame, California
Tel: 650-548-5386
www.europeanturkishmarket.com

Restaurants

Annie's Slovenian Restaurant
8430 Mayfield Road,
Chesterland, Ohio 44026
Tel: 440-729-4540

Bobak's
5275 South Archer Avenue,
Southwest Side, Chicago
Tel: 773-735-5334

Deta's Pita
7555 North Ridge Boulevard,
Far North Side, Chicago
Tel: 773-973-1505

Lutnia
5532 West Belmont Avenue,
Humboldt Park/Logan Square,
Chicago
Tel: 773-282-5335

Old L'Viv
2228 West Chicago Avenue,
Ukrainian Village/West Town,
Chicago
Tel: 773-772-7250

Paprikash
602 West Northwest Highway,
Arlington Heights, Illinois
Tel: 847-253-3544

Koliba
31-11 23rd Avenue, Queens,
New York NY 11105
Tel: 718-626-0430

Index

Bibliography
Bread Treasures of Slovenia by
J. Bogataj, ČZD Kmečki Glas
(Ljubljana 2003)
*European Cookery: Tradition
and Innovation*, L'Europe à
Table, Dutch Culinary Art
Foundation (Utrecht 2004)
Wines of Slovenia by
J. Namanič and J. Bogataj,
Rokus Gifts (Ljubljana 2004)
The Cuisine of Slovenia by
J. Bogataj, J. Nemanic and
S. Adamlje, Rokus Gifts
(Ljubljana 2005)
*Culinary Cultures of Europe:
Identity, Diversity and Dialogue*,
Council of Europe Publishing
(Strasbourg 2005)
Sweet Europe by J. Bogataj,
ČZD Kmečki Glas (Ljubljana
2007)
Taste Slovenia by J. Bogataj,
Rokus Gifts and National
Geographic (Ljubljana 2007)

**Publisher's
acknowledgements**

The publishers would like to
thank the following for
permission to reproduce their
images: p6 istockphoto; p7t
David Robertson/Alamy; p8
Cro Magnon/Alamy; p9tl Ladi
Kirn/Alamy; p9tr Superclic/
Alamy; p9b istockphoto; p10
Mitja Mladkovic/Alamy; p11b
R1/Alamy; p12l and p12m
istockphoto; p12r Blickwinkel/
Alamy; p13l and 13r
Imagebroker/Alamy
t=top, b=bottom, r=right, l=left,
m=middle. All other
photographs © Anness
Publishing Ltd.